THE TRUE COUNTRY

Flannery O'Connor and self-portrait

The True Country ❧ THEMES

IN THE FICTION OF

FLANNERY O'CONNOR

by CARTER W. MARTIN

VANDERBILT UNIVERSITY PRESS

The author and publisher gratefully acknowledge permission to quote from the following copyrighted material:

A Good Man Is Hard to Find and Other Stories, copyright © 1953, 1954, 1955 by Flannery O'Connor. Reprinted by permission of Harcourt, Brace & World, Inc.

Wise Blood, copyright © 1949, 1952, 1962 by Flannery O'Connor. *The Violent Bear It Away,* copyright © 1955, 1960 by Flannery O'Connor. *Everything That Rises Must Converge,* copyright © 1956, 1957, 1958, 1960, 1961, 1962, 1964, 1965 by the Estate of Mary Flannery O'Connor. "The Partridge Festival," copyright © 1961 by the Estate of Mary Flannery O'Connor. Reprinted with the permission of Farrar, Straus & Giroux, Inc.

The Living Novel: A Symposium, edited by Granville Hicks, © The Macmillan Company 1957.

"The Church and the Fiction Writer," *America,* March 30, 1957, © American Press, Inc., 1957.

"Flannery O'Connor's Devil," by John Hawkes, *The Sewanee Review,* LXX, 3, © The University of the South, 1962.

Photograph by Joe McTyre, Atlanta *Journal-Constitution.* Reproduced by permission.

For Jane, Carter, and Douglas

Contents

Acknowledgments

I gratefully acknowledge the help given me by Professor Thomas Daniel Young and Professor Herschel Gower, of Vanderbilt University, who advised and encouraged me throughout my work on this book; Mrs. Frank Owsley, who directed me to several letters from Flannery O'Connor to Andrew Lytle; Mr. Lytle himself, who gave his permission for me to quote from the letters; the library staff at the University of Alabama in Huntsville, who borrowed books and journals for me through interlibrary loans; and Miss Janice Daniel, who typed for me skillfully and patiently.

Huntsville, Alabama   C. W. M.
August 1968

Preface to the Paperback Edition

As I read *The True Country* twenty-four years after its first publication, I am struck by my confident, unapologetic use of words like *heathen, redemption, atheist, faith, sin,* and all the other specifically Christian terms. They remind me of Hemingway's priest in *A Farewell to Arms* when he asks Frederick Henry to go to the Abruzzi, his home in the cold, high mountains: "There in my country it is understood that a man may love God. It is not a dirty joke." At Vanderbilt in 1955, I had read A. J. Ayer's *Language, Truth, and Logic,* my introduction to logical positivism, a system I found quite inadequate for my critical purposes. Many of my peers, either convinced or frightened by that approach, went to great lengths to invent new language for old spirituality. Looking back now, I am pleased I did not choose circumlocutions for my own traditional vocabulary.

My youth and innocence are evident in this book. There is an inevitable bluntness about straightforward thematic analysis compared to sophisticated theoretical scholarship. But Flannery O'Connor, too, declared herself to be "congenitally innocent of theory." Of course she was not, but she said so in the "Author's Note to the Second Edition" of *Wise Blood*, enunciating her understanding of her audience: "That belief in Christ is to some a matter of life and death has been a stumbling block for readers who would prefer to think it a matter of no great consequence." Without so much as a nod to W. K. Wimsatt, Jr., and M. C. Beardsley, she spoke clearly and often about her intentions as a writer. In one particularly interesting formulation of her Christian preoccupation, she says it is a position not "easy in these times to make transparent in fiction." Reading that now, I am struck by the word *transparent*, for it touches upon issues that are timely and important. Does *transparent* mean that in good fiction we can clearly see meaning, through language, or that we simply see through language as if it were not there at all? O'Connor even dramatized this dilemma. In *Wise Blood*, Hazel Motes angrily explains to Onnie Jay Holy: "There's no such thing as any new jesus. That ain't anything but a way to say something. . . . No such thing exists!" Of this, I am sure, A. J. Ayer would approve.

O'Connor is not easy to read. For all her confidence in her purpose and for all my presumption in explaining her belief in the stories, it is ultimately difficult to say what she meant in this or that instance. Meanings, semantics, character, and intention are scrambled—deliberately, I believe—to provoke unthinking readers to confront the issues presented by O'Connor in her attempts to formulate language that will adequately account for human experience. My own critical position in dealing with these matters was, and still is, in the mainstream of critical inquiry: I attempt to study the mechanisms of narrative language for the purpose of revealing some of its complexities of meaning and beauty.

When I wrote *The True Country*, there was a good deal of misunderstanding about O'Connor and very little true criticism. It seemed important then to clarify for readers that her work was essentially different from that of Erskine Caldwell, Truman Capote, Carson Mc-Cullers, Tennessee Williams, or most of the other southern writers whose fiction presented grotesque or violent events and characters in a sharply defined regional milieu. I focused, therefore, on her avowed Christian purpose by analyzing her themes. Even now, Christian matters remain the beginning place for serious readers of O'Connor's fiction. To a great extent, these preoccupations account for the extraordinary power of her stories, their remarkable permanence as legends, parables, and paradigms of life as it was and is. The usefulness of this book is as an introduction to those works, written by a remarkable woman, who is, regardless of my unseasoned claim to the contrary in 1969, a major American writer.

The amount of criticism on O'Connor since this first book-length study of her work appeared is in itself testament to her importance. Books, articles, tapes, films, symposia, festivals, art exhibits, historical markers, literary prizes, societies, and two periodicals have swelled the annual bibliographies. As early as the mid-seventies a prominent critic called in vain for a moratorium on all the organized attention given her work. So much has been written that Neil Scott of the Russell Library, Georgia College, is now compiling an O'Connor bibliography for G. K. Scott's Goldentree series. His is a daunting task.

All of O'Connor's primary works, including the remarkable letters, are now available in published form:

> *Mystery and Manners: Occasional Prose.* Edited by Sally and Robert Fitzgerald. New York: Farrar, Straus, and Giroux, 1969.
>
> *The Complete Stories.* Edited and with an Introduction by Robert Giroux. New York: Farrar, Straus, and Giroux, 1971.
>
> *The Habit of Being: The Letters of Flannery O'Connor.* Edited and Introduced by Sally Fitzgerald. New York: Farrar, Straus, and Giroux, 1979.
>
> *The Presence of Grace and Other Book Reviews by Flannery O'Connor.* Compiled by Leo J. Zuber; Edited and Introduced by Carter W. Martin. Athens: University of Georgia Press, 1983.

Most of her manuscripts and papers are arranged, preserved, and available for study in the Flannery O'Connor Collection at Georgia College, in Milledgeville. Sally Fitzgerald's much anticipated biography will soon appear, and that will surely be the occasion for an outpouring of new critical appreciation.

Aside from the correction of several minor errors in the text, few changes have been made in this reissue of *The True Country.* If it were truly a revised edition, I would take more care over some of my aesthetic judgments and techniques of narrative. I would also change the now old-fashioned masculine pronoun references, though I would, of course, preserve O'Connor's use of them, as in her essay title, "The Fiction Writer and His Country."

On a personal note, I can say that the sympathy I came to experience for O'Connor's religious themes has affected me deeply and has sustained me in more ways than one. I am grateful to her for what she wrote and for the fortunate opportunity given me to devote much of my professional life to her achievement.

I wish to acknowledge the help and support of colleagues, friends, and family during the many years of my interest in Flannery O'Connor. I will never forget the hospitality and kindness of Mrs. Regina Cline O'Connor, and the good offices of Mr. Gerald Becham for introducing me to her. Sally Fitzgerald and her family, Thomas Daniel Young, the late Howell Daniel of the University of London, Sarah Gordon, editor of the *Flannery O'Connor Bulletin*, William Munson, John Conover, and innumerable colleagues who read and reviewed my work have all sustained and educated me. Finally, I owe a deep debt of gratitude to those who listened with love when I needed them: my mother, Martha; my son, Douglas; and my wife, Linda.

C. M.

Huntsville, Alabama

September 1993

Introduction

When Flannery O'Connor died in Milledgeville, Georgia, on August 3, 1964, at the age of thirty-nine she had achieved a substantial reputation as a writer of fiction on the basis of only three books and a number of stories. Her first published story, "The Geranium," appeared in 1946 in *Accent*. This was followed by the publication of *Wise Blood*, a novel, in 1952; *A Good Man Is Hard to Find*, a collection of ten short stories, in 1955; and in 1960 another novel, *The Violent Bear It Away*. A volume of stories, nine in all, was collected and published posthumously in 1965 under the title *Everything That Rises Must Converge*. Other works which do not appear in these books are two short stories, "The Capture" and "The Partridge Festival"; a very brief fragment of a novel, "Why Do the Heathens Rage?," published in *Esquire* (July 1963); *A Memoir of Mary Ann*, an introduction to an account by Catholic nuns of a child's experiences during her several years of living until cancer ended her life; an article in *Holiday* about peacocks, one of Miss

3

O'Connor's hobbies; and several reviews and critical pieces, concerned primarily with the responsibilities of the Christian writer.

On the basis of this relatively small amount of material, one would not be able to claim that Flannery O'Connor is a major modern writer. The quality of her fiction is such, however, that she must be considered an extremely important minor writer of national, even international, importance. In 1954 "The Life You Save May Be Your Own" was among the short stories in *The O. Henry Awards*; in the following decade, there were only three years in which one of her stories did not appear either in this collection or in one of the other important yearly prize collections, such as Martha Foley's *The Best Short Stories* or Paul Engle's *Prize Stories*. The years she was not represented, 1959–1961, were those in which the writing and publication of *The Violent Bear It Away* occupied her. In 1955 "A Circle in the Fire" was the second prize story in *The O. Henry Awards*; subsequently, two of her stories were chosen the best of the year—"Greenleaf" in 1957 and "Everything That Rises Must Converge" in 1963. Her works have been published outside the United States in Canada and England and have been translated into French, Greek, German, Japanese, and many other languages.

Critical attention to Flannery O'Connor's work has increased with the publication of each of her books and has reached a high point since her death. Early recognition of her talent is indicated by the stature of the periodicals in which her first stories appeared: between 1946 and 1952 her stories appeared in *Accent, Sewanee Review, Tomorrow, Mademoiselle, Partisan Review,* and *New World Writing*. Similarly, leading periodicals, both the large-circulation national magazines and book reviews and the small but influential scholarly journals, published reviews of *Wise Blood*. These reviews were not altogether sympathetic—some of them revealed total misunderstanding—but their very scope was an implicit recognition of Flannery O'Connor's importance as a writer. The publication of *A Good Man Is Hard to Find* was followed by more and better reviews, several of them treating this collection of stories along with Eudora Welty's *The Bride of Innisfallen* and showing critical understanding not apparent previously.

In 1957 Miss O'Connor published "The Fiction Writer and His Country" and "The Church and the Fiction Writer," two articles which set forth in unequivocal terms her personal beliefs as a writer. During the following year the first significant critical articles appeared in a special issue of *Critique* (Fall 1958) devoted exclusively to the work of Flannery O'Connor and J. F. Powers. In it appeared articles by Caroline Gordon, Louis D. Rubin, Jr., and Sister M. Bernetta Quinn, OSF, with a bibliography by George F. Wedge. During the next three years, the number of articles devoted to Miss O'Connor still was not appreciable, although the reviews of *The Violent Bear It Away* (1960) were abundant and showed more depth and sympathetic understanding than had been given to her other books. Since 1962, when several new articles not specifically reviews appeared, others have been published with increasing regularity. Recently two very helpful and incisive pamphlet studies—one by Robert

Drake and the other by Stanley Edgar Hyman—have added weight to this growing body of criticism. *The Added Dimension: The Mind and Art of Flannery O'Connor,* a collection of essays edited by Melvin J. Friedman and Lewis A. Lawson, appeared in 1966.

This book is valuable for its bibliography (complete to 1966), its collection of critical comments by Flannery O'Connor, and its impressive collection of essays. P. Albert Duhamel's contribution "The Novelist as Prophet" is particularly worthwhile insofar as Duhamel identifies an affinity between Flannery O'Connor and the Agrarians of *I'll Take My Stand;* like them she opposed the heresies of modernism and pleaded for a return to traditional values. Duhamel quotes directly from Allen Tate words which accord not only with Flannery O'Connor's beliefs but her fictional practice as well: "How may the Southerner take hold of his Tradition? . . . The answer is, by violence."[1] In "Flannery O'Connor's Testimony: The Pressure of Glory," Nathan A. Scott, Jr., makes essentially the same point about modernism, although he does not mention the Agrarians; Scott cites the contention of Mircea Eliade, the historian of religion, that present society differs from the traditional society primarily in its preference for a "basically desacralized cosmos."[2] Dulled modern man no longer feels the pressure of glory, as his anti-heroic, nihilistic literature makes clear; Scott argues that Flannery O'Connor not only portrayed that gray secu-

1. P. Albert Duhamel, "The Novelist as Prophet," *The Added Dimension: The Art and Mind of Flannery O'Connor,* edited by Melvin J. Friedman and Lewis A. Lawson, p. 104.
2. Nathan A. Scott, Jr., "Flannery O'Connor's Testimony: The Pressure of Glory," *ibid.,* p. 138.

lar world, but she presented it so violently as to arouse
the imagination and render it once again capable of
awe and receptive to magnificence.

Surveying the criticism, one finds a few biographical
articles, most of them personal reminiscences, some including correspondence. No full-length biography has
yet appeared, but Robert Fitzgerald, Miss O'Connor's
literary executor, is compiling the correspondence.
Some criticism has explored psychological and sociological matters relevant to the fiction, but in general this
sort of criticism is weak. Algene Ballif, for example,
considers *The Violent Bear It Away* to portray an inces-
tuous homosexual relationship;[3] Claire Rosenfield contends that old Mason Tarwater is insane, and like John
Hawkes she believes that Flannery O'Connor is on the
devil's side without knowing it.[4] There has not been
extensive investigation of literary influences, either contemporary or historical, although several articles and
reviews suggest that O'Connor's work is in the tradition
of American Gothic, having its roots in Poe and, perhaps more significantly, Hawthorne. Comparisons of
O'Connor with Capote and McCullers in this regard
have not been received favorably by the best critics of
her work. By far the greatest interest has been in
themes. Many critics and reviewers have questioned the
integrity of the novels artistically, contending that
O'Connnor is a short-story writer rather than a novelist,
but such aesthetic criticism has lacked extension.

3. Algene Ballif, "A Southern Allegory," *Commentary*, XXX
(October 1960) , 360.
4. Claire Rosenfield, "The Shadow Within: The Conscious
and Unconscious Use of the Double," in *Stories of the Double,*
edited by Albert J. Guerard, p. 325.

Scott, Duhamel, and other critics in *Art and Mind*
and elsewhere indicate that they consider Flannery
O'Connor's role as a novelist to be a prophetic one. She
herself was not reluctant to acknowledge her Christian
position as a writer. Knowing this, one may safely as-
sume that each of her stories is in some way informed by
a Christian point of view; he must not expect the sound-
ness of his assumption to simplify his analysis of her
work. The range of Christian themes is extensive and
the means of expressing them diverse. Miss O'Connor's
talent disposed her to employ techniques that were perplexing and even misleading at times: though a devout
Catholic, she portrayed fanatically Protestant characters and settings; her grotesque characters often were
more religious than normal people; and her sense of
universal charity and compassion was expressed in stories remarkable for their lack of sentimentality and
notable for wry and humorous satire. The resulting
complexity of her work requires the critic to proceed
with caution. The purpose of this thematic study is to
analyze Miss O'Connor's meanings by cutting across
chronological and generic lines for the purpose of isolat-
ing and defining the thematic tendencies in her work as
a whole. The first four chapters deal directly with the
religious content of the stories and novels, classifying
characters according to their functions in terms of the
religious themes, pointing out recurring conflicts, motifs, and plots. Chapters 5–8 attempt to identify the
thematic significance of characteristic features of Miss
O'Connor's fictional technique: her use of symbolism,
the grotesque, humor, and irony.

To make an extended study of themes in Flannery

O'Connor's fiction is to concentrate heavily on the aspect of fiction most important to her as a writer. It
seems significant and appropriate that her first published story, "The Geranium," appears again in revised
form in the posthumous volume, retitled "Judgement
Day" and standing last in the collection. Comparing
these stories, one is struck by the fact that "The Geranium" lacks not only the maturity and polish of the
later story but lacks also the forceful and bold inclusion
of an unmistakably Christian theme. Old Dudley in
"The Geranium" is entombed in his daughter's New
York apartment and is afraid to descend from it to
gather the broken remains of a cherished geranium
fallen to the street; old Tanner in "Judgement Day"
does not yield to the same kind of entombment and
symbolically rises from it by sheer strength of will and
belief that such entombment is terminable. At some
time between the publication of "The Geranium"
(Summer 1946) and the first published portion of *Wise
Blood* ("Train," April 1948), Flannery O'Connor implicitly committed herself as a writer to the Christian
theme; she pursued it with persistence and devotion
until her death. Any attempt at an appreciation of her
work must begin with a clear understanding of this
theme; regardless of one's own religious predilections,
he must know the meaning of the sacramental view of
life before he can know the meaning of Flannery
O'Connor's fiction. She fuses the transcendent world
with the sublunary one, achieving such a convergence
of actualities that one is meaningless without the other.

Chapter *1* The True
Country:
Flannery
O'Connor's
Sacramental
View

FLANNERY O'CONNOR'S
religious faith engages the interest of nearly every critic
or reviewer who considers her fiction. One is tempted to
conclude that this interest arises from the fact that she is
a Roman Catholic, since writers who happen to be
twentieth-century Methodists or Presbyterians rarely
provoke readers to consideration of their beliefs or the
extent to which doctrines peculiar to their faiths are
embodied in their fiction. The Roman Catholic who
writes fiction is the subject of extensive inquiry by those
who wish to demonstrate a novel or short story's orthodoxy or lack of it; by those who wish to instruct and
proselytize through criticism; and by those who, with
indignant alarm, feel that the writer is "up to something," especially if nothing in the work is patently
fashioned upon Roman Catholic doctrine. These latter
inquirers resemble certain characters from O'Connor's
novels and stories, such as Mrs. Shortley in "The Displaced Person," who fears the Polish immigrant Mr.
Guizac for the same reason that she fears the priest

responsible for bringing the man to the farm: "Mrs. Shortley looked at the priest and was reminded that these people did not have an advanced religion." She is aware that "They got the same religion as a thousand years ago."[1]

Some critics feel that a writer who is a Roman Catholic is as anachronistic as Mrs. Shortley finds the priest and Mr. Guizac. Philip Wylie, for example, states that "a Catholic, if he is devout, i.e., sold on the authority of his Church, is also brain-washed, whether he realizes it or not."[2] The Roman Catholic is often singled out in this fashion, and it is significant that the condition, "if he is devout," is either spelled out or implied. The attitude would seem to give general credence to the non-Catholic or to one who has fallen by the wayside, a "lapsed Catholic," as one of O'Connor's characters described himself, but not to one who believes in the doctrine and dogma of his church. Devout faith in the mysteries of Christianity is suspect, but the framework of Christianity, the body of Christian myth, its symbols, its prophecies, and its sacraments contribute the vocabulary most used by contemporary critics to describe the themes and structure of literature of all kinds. Often the writers themselves, through their heavily allusive mode, give the cue for such interpretation. And yet the works are not Christian in the theological sense. Although these works reveal an essentially Christian ethic,

---

1. Flannery O'Connor, *A Good Man Is Hard to Find,* pp. 202, 214. Further quotations from this work will be identified with the abbreviation *Good Man* and a page number in parentheses.

2. Quoted by Flannery O'Connor, "The Church and the Fiction Writer," *America,* March 30, 1957, p. 733.

an elaboration of the Sermon on the Mount, they do not demonstrate an orthodox Christian belief in God the Father, Jesus Christ, and the Holy Ghost. Such fiction, poetry, or drama, accepting the symbol but not the mystery, should not be misconstrued as Christian.

All Christian writers are certainly not Roman Catholics; our time, however, is one in which the latitude of belief in "advanced religion" makes it difficult to determine when a writer employs religious motifs from a secular point of view and not as an adjunct to devout faith. If the writer is a Catholic, this difficulty vanishes for many readers. The Catholic writer is assumed to be orthodox in his belief, whereas the Protestant or the writer who is a believer in religion without revelation is not expected to be orthodox. When the fiction of the latter writers refers to the religious view, one can take his choice between orthodox faith in God or a variety of ethical, psychological, or social meanings for which religious terminology is merely the cipher. Graham Greene, Evelyn Waugh, Francois Mauriac, and J. F. Powers are constantly cited and discussed as Catholic writers and measured against the beliefs of the church, while the Baptists and the Presbyterians escape such scrutiny under the aegis of "advanced religion."

Because of Flannery O'Connor's Catholicism, one is led to ask whether her Christian outlook affected her artistic vision and whether specific doctrines of the Roman Catholic Church find expression in her fiction.

The first question is easily and fully answered by Miss O'Connor's own generous explanations of her position. "When people have told me," she says in "The Church and the Fiction Writer," "that because I am Catholic, I cannot be an artist, I have had to reply, ruefully, that because I am a Catholic I cannot afford to be less than an artist."[3] She means several things by this answer. First (as she replied to a student who asked to know her reasons for writing), what she does best must be done for God: "There is no excuse, however excellent, for anyone to write fiction for public consumption unless he has been called to do so by the presence of a gift. . . . A gift of any kind is a considerable responsibility. It is a mystery in itself, something gratuitous and wholly undeserved."[4]

Another meaning attached to her answer is deeper— that as a Catholic her vision is directed by a sacramental view of life. In a lecture delivered at Notre Dame University, she said, "The Catholic sacramental view of life is one that maintains and supports at every turn the vision that the story teller must have if he is going to write fiction of any depth."[5] This view invests each moment and even the most insignificant event with an importance worthy of its being shaped and given form through the medium of art. O'Connor contends that fiction "should reinforce our sense of the supernatural by grounding it in concrete observable reality."[6] She achieves this combination of the supernatural and the

3. *Ibid.,* p. 734.
4. Quoted by Rosa Lee Walston, "Flannery O'Connor—A Good Writer Is Hard to Find," *Columns* (The Woman's College of Georgia), Fall 1965, p. 11.
5. Quoted by Robert Fitzgerald, "Introduction," Flannery O'Connor, *Everything That Rises Must Converge,* p. xxiv.
6. O'Connor, "The Church and the Fiction Writer," p. 734.

concrete in a great variety of ways; at one extreme she uses the traditional symbols of the sun, light and dark, and such animals as the peacock to link the rural landscape of her stories with the eternal landscape, "the true country." The same bridge is made, however, when her images are drawn from the ordinary features of commonplace lives; "it is her particular genius," Richard Poirier remarks, "to make us believe that there are Christian mysteries in things irreduceably [*sic*] banal. And in this too there is an aspect of Catholicism, most beautifully exemplified in the penultimate stanza of the 'Paradiso,' where Dante likens his poetic efforts in fashioning a vision of God to the work of a 'good tailor.' "[7] A worthy example of this talent is found in the imagery of one of her most memorable and arresting titles, "The Artificial Nigger," a short story in which a crude statue of a Negro boy effects a reconciliation between a grandfather and the grandson he betrayed: "They stood gazing at the artificial Negro as if they were faced with some great mystery, some monument to another's victory that brought them together in their common defeat. They could both feel it dissolving their differences like an action of mercy" (*Good Man*, pp. 127–128). Incidents equally remarkable are found throughout the novels and stories.

The sacramental view is, of course, more than the transformation of an object into a sign of the mystery that resides in the created universe; as the term itself says, it is a vision of reality focused through the seven sacraments which constitute the means of recognizing

7. "If You Know Who You Are You Can Go Anywhere," *New York Times Book Review*, May 30, 1965, p. 6.

and accepting divine grace. The sacramental view thus provides for man's discovery of his place in the divine scheme of salvation—the recognition and acceptance of grace, an event that in O'Connor's fiction can be as quiet and subtle as that of Mr. Head and Nelson, as violent as that of Mrs. May in "Greenleaf" when she is gored by a mad bull, or as direct and insistent as that of Mrs. Turpin in "Revelation," who sees in the late evening sky "a vast horde of souls . . . rumbling toward heaven."[8] The major characters in most of the stories and in the two novels are brought to the realization of their own guilt and inadequacy and to the consequent discovery that their heretofore unacknowledged and perpetual sin throws upon them the need to join the vast horde and accept the grace offered through the vision. "We lost our innocence in the fall of our first parents," she remarks in "The Church and the Fiction Writer," "and our return to it is through the redemption which was brought about by Christ's death and by our slow participation in it."[9]

The very title of her posthumously published volume of short stories, *Everything That Rises Must Converge,* expresses Flannery O'Connor's constant concern with man's "slow participation" in redemption. The title is taken from the writings of a Jesuit priest, Pierre Teilhard de Chardin, "whose works Flannery O'Connor had been reading at least since early 1961,"[10] and whose

8. Flannery O'Connor, *Everything That Rises Must Converge,* p. 217. Further quotations from this work will be identified with the abbreviation *Everything* and a page number in parentheses.
9. P. 734.
10. Fitzgerald, *op. cit.,* p. xxx.

ideas are highly relevant to the particular meaning of
Flannery O'Connor's sacramental view. Teilhard's *The
Phenomenon of Man* expresses his belief in an evolutionary process toward an ultimate Omega point, at
which the consciousness of the self (hominisation, "the
individual and instantaneous leap from instinct to
thought . . . [and] the progressive phyletic spiritualiza-
tion in human civilization of all the forces contained in
the animal world"[11]) is coincident with, but not contra-
dictory to, an absorption into the Oneness of universal
energy, both physical and psychical, which exists beyond the organic multiplicity of the past. Basing his
opinions on biology, physics, archaeology—upon all
fields of science—Teilhard demonstrates the existence
of an evolutionary force in even the lowest forms of life
driving them toward ever-increasing complexity, rising
toward the phenomenon of man. Because space and
time contain and engender consciousness, they are "nec-
essarily *of a convergent nature*"[12] and productive of
higher forms of spiritual life.

Such ideas as Teilhard's may not on the surface seem
appreciably different from those of Bergson or of Sir
Julian Huxley, as Huxley himself points out in his
introduction to *The Phenomenon of Man;* Teilhard in
his preface to the same book asks that it be read as a
scientific treatise and not as a theological essay or as a
work on metaphysics.[13] Yet he explains in the epilogue,
"The Christian Phenomenon," that Christianity is the

11. Pierre Teilhard de Chardin, *The Phenomenon of Man,* p.
180.
  12. *Ibid.,* p. 259.
  13. *Ibid.,* p. 29.

most potent manifestation of hominisation, of rising and convergence. In the essay itself he insists upon the importance in the scheme of individual, personal recognitions which contribute to the general upward movement of the phylum. The universe builds itself from thought, which moves in an upward direction, opposite to the movement of matter. "The universe is a collector and conservator, not of mechanical energy . . . , but of persons."[14] Separate souls carry their consciousness upward but become synthesized at the Omega point, at which the convergent nature of the universe is achieved.

Just as Teilhard's system encompasses the slow time of prehistory leading to the emergence of man, Flannery O'Connor's fiction gives dramatic, concrete form to the humble and often banal insight that enables the individual man to move toward grace by rising only slightly. It is *this* movement that she means when she speaks of our slow participation in redemption. Flannery O'Connor's recognition of this very real phenomenon of rising and converging is at the heart of her own sacramental view. Yet there is no systematic, allegorical representation of Teilhard's ideas in her fiction.

The dangers inherent in a detailed comparison of Teilhard's ideas with Flannery O'Connor's themes are equally present in any attempt to interpret her stories in the context of predetermined Catholic theology. In regard to her religious position as a writer, she says in "The Fiction Writer and His Country":

I am no disbeliever in spiritual purpose and no vague believer. I see from the standpoint of Christian orthodoxy.

14. *Ibid.,* p. 272.

This means that for me the meaning of life is centered in our Redemption by Christ and that what I see in the world I see in its relation to that. I don't think that this is a position that can be taken halfway or one that is particularly easy in these times to make transparent in fiction.[15]

Too many readers of Flannery O'Connor, or any openly orthodox Catholic writer, move from one premise to the next to arrive at the conclusion that a Catholic writer who is orthodox is a perpetrator of systematic Roman Catholic theology. Most unbiased critics, however, point out, as Caroline Gordon does, that the "theological framework is never explicit in Miss O'Connor's fiction."[16] Sister Mariella Gable says that "She wrote for an unbelieving world, not for Catholics."[17]

It is, of course, from the statements of Flannery O'Connor herself that her attitude toward the doctrines of the church can best be understood. In them she insists time and again upon the integrity of the fiction according to its own determinants. In an interview at the Vanderbilt Literary Symposium in 1959, she said that the writer should not "begin a story with a system. You can forget about the system. These are things that you believe; they may affect your writing unconsciously. I don't think theology should be a scaffolding."[18] She

15. Flannery O'Connor, "The Fiction Writer and His Country," *The Living Novel: A Symposium,* edited by Granville Hicks, p. 162.

16. "Flannery O'Connor's *Wise Blood,*" *Critique,* II (Fall 1958), 9.

17. "Flannery O'Connor: A Tribute," *Esprit* [University of Scranton], VIII (Winter 1964), 26.

18. "An Interview with Flannery O'Connor and Robert Penn Warren," *Vagabond* [Vanderbilt University], IV (February 1960), 14.

contends that the writer who is Catholic must protect himself from a false conception of the demands of the church's dogma; the writer who dwells upon this concern to the extreme is in danger of reaching an impasse, having to choose between writing what could possibly "lead the reader into sin," and, on the other hand, not writing at all. Such a dilemma is avoided by her understanding that the writer must "limit himself to the concerns proper to what he is creating." She expresses it this way:

> The limitations that any writer imposes on his work will grow out of the necessities that lie in the material itself, and these will generally be more rigorous than any that religion could impose. Part of the complexity of the problem for the Catholic fiction-writer will be the presence of grace as it appears in nature, and what matters for him here is that his faith not become detached from his dramatic sense and from his vision of what is. No one in these days, however, would seem more anxious to have it become detached than those Catholics who demand that the writer limit, on the natural level, what he allows himself to see.[19]

A writer who would compromise his art in the name of church doctrine is, in her opinion, the victim of "a sorry education" or not a writer in the first place. But such a position, she admits, might well have been "foisted on him by the general atmosphere of Catholic piety in this country."[20]

What can be seen clearly, then, in her statements concerning the Catholic writer and in her short stories and novels is that she is not conscious of being a Roman

19. O'Connor, "The Church and the Fiction Writer," p. 734.
20. *Ibid.*

Catholic when she writes; she accepts her Christian
orthodoxy as naturally as if schisms had never occurred,
as seriously and sometimes as stringently as if she were a
contemporary of Geoffrey Chaucer rather than of John
O'Hara. Perhaps this lack of religious self-consciousness
has something to do with the fact that she was born to
it; as Kathleen Knott observes in *The Emperor's
Clothes,* "It seems to be much easier for Catholic writers
who are born Catholic, for instance Mauriac, to stick to
psychological truth than it is for converts. This may be
because it is much easier to ignore Catholic theory
when it is acquired below the age of reason."[21]
O'Connor's inclusion of Roman Catholics in her stories
is infrequent and then almost coincidental; she does not
rely, as Graham Greene often does, upon a Roman
Catholic in her stories to point up the religious view of
the church. Indeed, her most important religious characters are nearly always Protestants, often of the most
aberrant kind. The effectiveness of her use of such characters arises from her ecumenical religious position,
which has been analyzed in an article by Sister Mariella
Gable, "The Ecumenic Core in the Fiction of Flannery
O'Connor."[22] Flannery O'Connor specifically approved
of this article, saying in a letter to the sister, "I am more
and more impressed with the amount of Catholicism
that fundamentalist Protestants have been able to retain.
Theologically our differences with them are on the nature of the Church, not on the nature of God or our ob-
ligations to Him."[23] In the same lengthy letter she ex-

21. Quoted in A. A. DeVitis, *Graham Greene,* p. 42.
22. *American Benedictine Review,* XV (June 1964), 127–143.
23. Letter to Sister Mariella Gable, May 4, 1963, as quoted in
Gable, *loc. cit.*

plains to Sister Mariella that she must describe in her fiction what she sees, not what is socially or theologically desirable to the typical Catholic reader. And she explains, too, another reason for her frequent use of Protestants as her major characters:

And the fanatics. People make a judgment of fanticism by what they are themselves. To a lot of Protestants I know, monks and nuns are fanatics, none greater. And to a lot of monks and nuns I know, my Protestant prophets are fanatics. For my part, I think the only difference between them is that if you are a Catholic and have this intensity of belief you join the convent and are heard no more; whereas if you are a Protestant and have it, there is no convent for you to join and you go about the world getting into all sorts of trouble and drawing the wrath of people who don't believe anything much at all down on your head.

This is one reason why I can write about Protestant believers better than Catholic believers—because they express their belief in diverse kinds of dramatic action which is obvious enough for me to catch. I can't write about anything subtle.[24]

It would seem apparent, then, that the questions posed by Flannery O'Connor's religious faith may be answered by saying that she writes from an orthodox Christian point of view but grinds no theological ax, unless the basic Christian truth of man's fall from grace and his redemption through Christ's sacrifice be so construed. She depicts man's fallen state in a procession of characters who are proud, mean, intolerant, ignorant, and generally sinful; but to each is offered the opportunity of salvation.

All of the stories, of course, are not religiously oriented. Some few, such as "A Late Encounter With the

24. *Ibid.,* pp. 26–27.

Enemy" and, perhaps, "The Comforts of Home," are religious only in the broadest sense; it is unlikely that a reader not familiar with Flannery O'Connor's other work would find even that general religious implication. Others ("A Stroke of Good Fortune" and "A View of the Woods") lend themselves readily to analysis through religious terminology and are relevant to such a point of view but do not require it. A large number of stories demand attention to their religious significance, even though the action does not specifically relate to the characters' consideration of it. In such stories, the Christian theme is designated by the title of the story or by certain allusions or clearly allegorical situations; "A Circle in the Fire," "The Artificial Nigger," "Greenleaf," "Everything That Rises Must Converge," and "Judgement Day" are in this category. Nearly all the other stories may be categorized on the basis of their open concern with religious themes: the characters do not know God, they knowingly perpetrate blasphemy, they are in flight from God, or they come to recognize God for the first time. The two novels, *Wise Blood* and *The Violent Bear It Away,* are in this last category, as are "A Good Man Is Hard to Find," "The River," "A Temple of the Holy Ghost," "Good Country People," and "The Displaced Person" from *A Good Man Is Hard to Find;* "The Enduring Chill," "The Lame Shall Enter First," "Revelation," and "Parker's Back," appearing in *Everything That Rises Must Converge.*

Miss O'Connor's sacramental view surveys the countryside and illuminates it so that her readers may see the true country in it and above it; the outward features and the natural actions are the signs of inward and spiritual grace, as they are in "Judgement Day," a story which begins in tawdriness and ends in joy. Old T. C. Tanner's[25] daughter finds him living in a squalid shack in Corinth, Georgia, with his constant Negro companion, Coleman Parrum; the daughter insists that Tanner leave Coleman and return home to New York with her. There, in an apartment with his daughter and her insensitive, atheistic truck-driver husband, the old man longs to be back in Corinth; as a result of his longing for home, he attempts to befriend a Negro tenant, as he had Coleman Parrum. This Negro, however, is cynical, atheistic, and proud; Tanner's innocent patronizing antagonizes the Negro and sets in motion the events which lead to Tanner's first stroke. When the old man learns that his daughter intends, against his wishes, to bury him not in Corinth but in New York, he begins planning, in spite of his illness, his return to his true country in the South. He dies of a second stroke on the first flight of stairs, where he is found by the Negro actor who furiously lodges the old man in the banister rungs because he misinterprets Tanner's appeal to Coleman as a mocking epithet, coal-man.

As the title might indicate, "Judgement Day" has strong allegorical overtones. As is often true of the city in Flannery O'Connor's fiction, New York is a place of the damned, a godless hell for the old man, allegorically a purgatory of suffering antecedent to his entry into the

25. In the two instances in which his name appears, he signs T. C. Tanner in one, W. T. Tanner in the other; although one is tempted to search for some symbolic significance in this discrepancy, relating to the theme of identity and the story's recurrent motif of the *Doppelgänger,* it would seem instead to be simply an oversight in proofreading.

eternal true country. Tanner's thoughts move from
those of his imprisonment in the "pigeon-hutch of a
building," to those of Coleman and Corinth, and to
those of Judgment Day:

[Tanner's daughter] sat there silently a few moments. Then
she began. "The trouble with you is," she said, "you sit in
front of that window all the time where there's nothing to
look out at. You need some inspiration and an out-let. If
you would let me pull your chair around to look at the TV,
you would quit thinking about morbid stuff, death and hell
and judgement. My Lord."

"The Judgement is coming," he muttered. "The sheep'll
be separated from the goats. Them that kept their promises
from them that didn't. Them that did the best they could
with what they had from them that didn't. Them that honored their father and their mother from them that cursed
them. Them that . . ." (*Everything,* pp. 257–258) .

The theme of the story is the certainty of resurrection
at Judgment Day for those who kept their promises, did
their best, and honored their parents. Clearly, this reci-
tation is a fragment of Tanner's colloquial rendering of
the Ten Commandments and the Beatitudes. Later in
the story, when Tanner realizes the imminence of his
death just before falling down the stairs, he quotes
" 'The Lord is my shepherd, . . . I shall not want' " (p.
267) . Though the conclusion of this psalm is not sup-
plied, its meaning is so strongly felt that its inclusion is
not necessary: "And I will dwell in the house of the
Lord for ever" (Ps. 23:6) .

Tanner defends his faith when it is reviled by the
Negro actor, who says:

"I don't take no crap . . . off no wool-hat red-neck son-of-a-
bitch peckerwood old bastard like you." He caught his

breath. And then his voice came out in the sound of an exasperation so profound that it rocked on the verge of a laugh. It was high and piercing and weak. "And I'm not no preacher! I'm not even no Christian. I don't believe that crap. There ain't no Jesus and there ain't no God."

The old man felt his heart inside him hard and tough as an oak knot. "And you ain't black," he said. "And I ain't white!" (*Everything,* p. 263).

The old man not only expresses an equation between the mystery of man's identity and the mystery of God's being, but he is, in this example, an illustration of Christ's pronouncement in the Beatitudes:

> Blessed are ye, when men shall revile you, and persecute you, and shall say all manner of evil against you falsely, for my sake. Rejoice, and be exceeding glad: for great is your reward in heaven: for so persecuted they the prophets which were before you (Matt. 5:1–12).

Further, T. C. Tanner has followed Christ's teaching that one should love his neighbor as himself. In an almost Christlike manner, he has assumed the responsibility for Coleman Parrum for thirty years after seeing the Negro, triumphed over by Tanner at their first meeting, as "a negative image of himself, as if clownishness and captivity had been their common lot" (p. 255). Although Tanner tells his daughter that Coleman is paroled to him, the bond which joins them is more than a legal one—it is moral and spiritual.

Tanner wants his body sent to Coleman if he dies en route to Corinth, and to ensure that he arrives there, the old man pins this note inside his coat pocket:

IF FOUND DEAD SHIP EXPRESS COLLECT TO COLEMAN PARRUM, CORINTH, GEORGIA. Under this he had continued: COLEMAN

SELL MY BELONGINGS AND PAY THE FREIGHT ON ME & THE UN-
DERTAKER. ANYTHING LEFT OVER YOU CAN KEEP YOURS TRULY
T.C. TANNER. P.S. STAY WHERE YOU ARE DON'T LET THEM TALK
YOU INTO COMING UP HERE. ITS NO KIND OF PLACE (p. 246).

Tanner's only concern, other than for Coleman's welfare, is that he arrive where he wishes to be: "Dead or
alive. It was being there that mattered; the dead or
alive did not" (p. 246).

The old man's resurrection is anagogically indicated
in his dream concerning his death and the shipment of
him in his coffin to Corinth. In his dream he is alive in
the pine box, aware of "the cold early morning air of
home coming in through the cracks," and aware too of
Coleman and Hooten, the station agent, sorrowful and
red-eyed, unloading the box:

From inside he began to scratch on the wood.
    They let go as if it had caught fire.
    They stood looking at each other, then at the box.
    "That him," Coleman said. "He in there his self."
    "Naw," Hooten said, "must be a rat got in there with
him."
    "That him. This here one of his tricks."
    "If it's a rat he might as well stay."
    "That him. Git a crowbar."
Hooten went grumbling off and got the crowbar and
came back and began to pry open the lid. Even before he
had the upper end pried open, Coleman was jumping up
and down, wheezing and panting from excitement. Tanner
gave a thrust upward with both hands and sprang up in the
box. "Judgement Day! Judgement Day!" he cried. "Don't
you two fools know it's Judgement Day?" (p. 265).

This dream of arising from the coffin into the true
country of his life, Corinth, Georgia, to be reunited
with those he cares for is repeated in Tanner's delirium

on the stairs when he thinks the Negro actor is Coleman; its repetition insistently calls for a symbolic interpretation in which real death is followed by the resurrection of the body. Such an interpretation is appropriate, too, for the story's concluding event, in which Tanner's daughter, having buried her father against his wishes in New York, has him exhumed and shipped back to Corinth.

The remarkable achievement of "Judgement Day" is its unmistakable evocation of joy and spiritual triumph out of material that is otherwise pathetic, ugly, and violent; Flannery O'Connor's sacramental view of humanity throughout her fiction focuses upon such transformations.

Chapter 2 The
Countryside:
Corruptions
of the
Spirit

ALTHOUGH T. C. Tan-
ner is saved and his story is thus ultimately happy, there
is no prettiness in "Judgement Day"; Tanner's symbolic yearning for grace is made emphatic by the contrast provided by the urban image of hell and the character foils of the truck driver and the Negro actor. Such
characters far outnumber the Tanners in Miss
O'Connor's stories and novels; they run the gamut of
corruption: religious ignorance, moral blindness and
self-righteousness, outlandish deceit and hypocrisy, cynicism, hedonism, outright atheism, and evil so profound
as to be nothing less than satanic. The proliferation of
such characters gives a flavor to Flannery O'Connor's
work which has horrified some critics and readers; to
them it would perhaps seem surprising that the spiritually unsound characters and the thoroughly evil ones
should be the starting place for the consideration of the
religious content of Miss O'Connor's fiction. Her own
comment supplies the rationale for beginning with
them: "The writer has to make the corruption believa-

ble before he can make the grace meaningful."[1] God's grace is her chief subject: its presence and recognition in the lives of some; its rejection and absence in the lives of many.

In its most ordinary, banal, and universal manifestation, the fallen condition of man appears in those who are ignorant of grace because of complacency, self-righteousness, and pride. They are created by Flannery O'Connor as people who are not violently or grandly sinful, nor even perverse, devious, and secretive. They are merely fools.

Although the invincibly ignorant may not be specifically evil, they have not the slightest inclination toward the religious point of view; aware of its existence, they have no desire to know more about it. In *The Violent Bear It Away* George F. Rayber's father is the epitome of the type. It is his blood, his influence which determine the irreligious nature of George Rayber, the schoolteacher (whose mother was old Mason Tarwater's sister, described by him as a whore who left her birthplace, Powderhead, Tennessee, at eighteen and finally found a man who would marry her, the elder Rayber). This character is not merely incidental to the narrative, for his description clearly indicates the extensive effect of his religious ignorance:

The man, an insurance salesman, wore a straw hat on the side of his head and smoked a cigar and when you told him

1. Sister Mariella Gable, "Flannery O'Connor: A Tribute," *Esprit* [University of Scranton], VIII (Winter 1964), p. 26.

his soul was in danger, he offered to sell you a policy against any contingency. He said he was a prophet too, a prophet of life insurance, for every right-thinking Christian, he said, knew that it was his Christian duty to protect his family and provide for them in the event of the unexpected. There was no use treating with him, the old man said; his brain was as slick as his eyeballs and the truth would no more soak into it than rain would penetrate tin. The schoolteacher, with Tarwater blood in him, at least had his father's strain diluted.[2]

Unlike his son George, who resists Tarwater's wish to baptize his idiot son Bishop, the elder Rayber, attaching not the slightest religious significance to the forms of Christianity, was unmoved a generation earlier when old Mason Tarwater kidnapped George and baptized him. When the child George explained to his father with conviction, "I've been born again," the elder Rayber's reply was the height of religious insensitivity: "Great . . . , Great. . . . Glad you got him fixed up Mason. . . . One bath more or less won't hurt the bugger" (*Violent*, p. 127) . The legacy of his father's ignorance is indicated by Rayber's mature godlessness and his choice of a wife, Bernice Bishop, a social worker who surrenders the infant Tarwater to his great uncle and abandons her husband and their son because the child is a congenital idiot. The elder Rayber's ignorance threw him upon the salvation of life insurance; hers embraced the doctrines of social welfare. These characters and Sheppard, the recreation director in "The Lame Shall Enter First," are insensitive to God's grace and fall upon some

2. Flannery O'Connor, *The Violent Bear It Away*, p. 59. Further quotations from this work will be identified with the abbreviation *Violent* and a page number in parentheses.

form of secular "enlightenment" as a replacement for it.

The absence of grace is shown in a different form in those who are aware enough of religious values and believe in them, but who fail to act upon their belief or to see a correlation between it and the moral problems that confront them. Mrs. McIntyre in "The Displaced Person," Mrs. Cope in "A Circle in the Fire," and Joanne and Susan, the adolescent girls in "A Temple of the Holy Ghost," are like Aunt Bessie and Aunt Mattie in "The Partridge Festival": "They were both good low-church Episcopalians but they had amoral imaginations."[3]

Mrs. McIntyre, the owner of the farm where the action of "The Displaced Person" takes place, is not presented as a religious figure; but she has a strong sense of what is, in her personal interpretation, right. Like many other O'Connor characters, her morality depends heavily upon trite aphorisms. Most of these she attributes to the Judge, her first husband, whom she married for money "when she was thirty and he was seventy-five." Although he left her almost nothing when he died, she revered the Judge as the source of truths such as: "One fellow's misery is the other fellow's gain," "The devil you know is better than the devil you don't," "You couldn't have your pie and eat it too," and "Money is the root of all evil."[4] She is similar to Mrs.

3. Flannery O'Connor, "The Partridge Festival," reprinted in *The Sense of Fiction,* Welker and Gower, editors, p. 374.
4. Flannery O'Connor, *A Good Man Is Hard to Find,* pp. 216, 224. Further quotations from this work will be identified with the abbreviation *Good Man* and a page number in parentheses.

Shortley, the wife of the dairyman in the same story, who suspects the priest because he does not have an "advanced religion." As Robert Fitzgerald has remarked, Mrs. McIntyre's religion is "so far reformed that no nonsense at all remains. It is a managerial religion, the one by which daily business in a realm gets done."[5] Her chief concerns in life are money, her property and possessions, and what she considers her upright image in the eyes of others. Her words ring with religious conviction when she tells Astor, the old Negro on her place, that "only the smart thrifty energetic ones are going to survive." And when the old priest who visits her talks about purgatory, she declares proudly that she is practical, not theological. Later, he attempts to draw a parallel between Mr. Guizac's situation and that of "Christ Our Lord," and Mrs. McIntyre protests in exasperation, "I'm a logical practical woman and there are no ovens here and no camps and no Christ Our Lord and when he leaves, he'll make more money" (*Good Man*, p. 245).

Just as Mrs. Shortley's vision indicates to her the demise of the hated Mr. Guizac when "The children of wicked nations will be butchered" (*Good Man*, pp. 218–219), "self-sufficient pragmatism"[6] thrusts upon Mrs. McIntyre the responsibility of firing him. Mr. Guizac's "monstrous crime" has been an attempt to marry Sulk, the young Negro worker, to Mr. Guizac's cousin in Europe in order to release her from a camp for displaced persons after World War II. Although Mrs.

5. "The Countryside and the True Country," *Sewanee Review,* LXX (Summer 1962), 389.
6. *Ibid.,* p. 394.

McIntyre is capable of a certain lukewarm pity toward him, Mr. Guizac is little more to her than an expendable and sometimes unreliable commodity, or at best someone who owes her a debt for having given him a job. "She was sorry that the poor man had been chased out of Poland and run across Europe and had had to take up in a tenant shack in a strange country, but she had not been responsible for any of this. . . . She had given him a job. She didn't know if he was grateful or not" (pp. 229–230). In trying to explain to him that one who calls himself a Christian would not try to marry an innocent child to "a half-witted thieving black stinking nigger," she brings her self-righteous moral position to a clear climax when she declares that she is "not responsible for the world's misery" (pp. 234–235).

In spite of all her later disclaimers, Mrs. McIntyre recognizes and admits early in the story that she does indeed owe something to Mr. Guizac. Not only does she indicate to Mrs. Shortley (not without some intent to threaten her and Mr. Shortley for their shiftlessness) that she would be willing gladly to increase Mr. Guizac's wages to keep him; she says that he has "saved" her and that "That man is my salvation" (p. 209). Mrs. Shortley observes that she has changed since Mr. Guizac arrived and "begun to act like somebody who was getting rich secretly" (p. 215). Clearly the displaced person allegorically represents an opportunity for Mrs. McIntyre to accept grace; and it is an opportunity that is first passed up in the name of morality and later violently disposed of when Mrs. McIntyre, Sulk, and Mr. Shortley tacitly assent to the death of Mr. Guizac as they watch silently, transfixed by their hatred of the man, while his body is crushed under the wheels of a tractor. The religious implications of her guilt are boldly shown by the continuing visits of the priest and the persistent Christian symbol of the peacock in contrast to the disintegration of her life. Mr. Shortley leaves, the Negroes abandon her, she is hospitalized with a nervous affliction, and the farm is sold by an auctioneer. These are the wages not of violent and perverse sins, but of the rejection of grace offered in the circumstances of life at its most ordinary level.

A similar moral failure occurs in "A Circle in the Fire," a story in which the name of the main character, Mrs. Cope, indicates her proud, selfish possessiveness. Like Mrs. McIntyre she has an intense conviction of her own benevolence and generosity. Ironically, her invocations in the name of the Lord are for protection from fire and the destructiveness of her Negroes and the nut grass; her prayers are thanksgiving for her possessions and for her general condition, comfortable enough to allow her pity for a woman who died with her newborn baby in an iron lung and for the poor Europeans, who serve more than once in Flannery O'Connor's stories as an object of pity sufficiently distant to require only charitable thoughts. Mrs. Cope is confronted with the opportunity to act out charity rather than meditate briefly upon it when Powell Boyd, the son of her former hired man who moved to the city, arrives with two companions, Garfield Smith and W. T. Harper. They are pinched, hungry, almost destitute children who come to the country to ride the horses that Powell has talked about constantly and to enjoy the outdoors. Although it is clear that the boys have a typically childish, idealized conception of Mrs. Cope's farm, the details of their attitude toward it indicate that Flannery O'Connor intends for the reader to see their symbolic sense of identity with this land. It is an earthly paradise and an eternal landscape to which their claim is as real as Mrs. Cope's. Not only has Powell told the others that "he had the best time of his entire life right here on this here place," he has said as well that "when he died he wanted to come here!" (*Good Man*, pp. 136–137). One of the other boys says that Powell "don't like it in Atlanta. . . . He ain't ever satisfied with where he's at except this place here" (p. 139). After Mrs. Cope realizes that the boys intend to ride the horses without her permission and that they intend to remain for several days, her charity, which consists of offering the boys some guinea, sandwiches, and crackers, wears thin to the point that she exclaims to Mrs. Pritchard and to the boys, "After all, . . . this is my place." Later they say to Mr. Pritchard, making their position quite clear and the symbolism obvious, "She don't own them woods. . . . Man, Gawd owns them woods and her too" (p. 145).

The boys take their revenge upon Mrs. Cope through various acts of vandalism, leading her to threaten to report them to the sheriff. The guilt in the story is not simple, for it is as much the boys' as it is Mrs. Cope's. But the religious point is drawn in terms of her failure to rise above her lack of generosity. Justice—as certain and as clearly identifiable as it is in Elizabethan drama—comes to her in the form of fire set by the boys in her woods. This traditional symbol of purgatorial purification is unmistakably indicated by the title of the story, "A Circle in the Fire." But to Mrs. Cope it is as signifi- cant as the nut grass and weeds which she considered to be "an evil sent directly by the devil to destroy the place." As the fire rages, Mrs. Cope's daughter looks at her mother's face and sees there the effect of the fire upon her:

The child came to a stop beside her mother and stared up at her face as if she had never seen it before. It was the face of the new misery she felt, but on her mother it looked old and it looked as if it might have belonged to anybody, a Negro or a European or to Powell himself. The child turned her head quickly, and past the Negroes' ambling fig- ures she could see the column of smoke rising and widening unchecked inside the granite line of trees. She stood taut, listening, and could just catch in the distance a few wild high shrieks of joy as if the prophets were dancing in the fiery furnace, in the circle the angel had cleared for them (p. 154).

The specifically Biblical point is made in the conclud- ing reference to the prophets in the fiery furnace. In the third chapter of the book of Daniel, Shadrach, Me- shach, and Abednego are cast into the fiery furnace by King Nebuchadnezzar when they refuse to bow down to the idol to which he directed their worship. The three are miraculously saved from the flames by a fourth figure in the furnace:

Then Nebuchadnezzar spake, and said, Blessed be the God of Shadrach, Meshach, and Abednego, who hath sent his angel, and delivered his servants that trusted in him, and have changed the king's word, and yielded their bodies, that they might not serve nor worship any god, except their own God. Therefore I make a decree, that every people, nation, and language, which speak any thing amiss against the God of Shadrach, Meshach, and Abednego, shall be cut in pieces, and their houses shall be made a dunghill: because there is no other God that can deliver after this sort (Dan. 3:28–29).

Like Nebuchadnezzar, Mrs. Cope has worshiped the golden image of her farm and has tried to force the boys to bow down to it; unlike the biblical king, she comes to no revelation as she witnesses the fiery event, for she feels only sorrow, loss, and misery.

"A Temple of the Holy Ghost" offers another example of the failure to accept grace clearly offered. The principal theme of the story is the sacrament of confirmation[7] from the point of view of a twelve-year-old girl. A subsidiary theme, however, is the contrasting blindness of the two fourteen-year-old girls Joanne and Susan, who are visiting from the convent school Mount St. Scholastica. While the mystical reality of the title is being made manifest to the younger child through the grotesque bodies of those around her, Joanne and Susan, past the age of confirmation, cannot understand the human body in any terms but those dictated by their rampant, emergent sexuality. Their adolescent, mindless blasphemy toward this sacrament is a serious matter treated in a ludicrous passage:

[The child's mother] asked them why they called each other Temple One and Temple Two and this sent them off into gales of giggles. Finally they managed to explain. Sister Perpetua, the oldest nun at the Sisters of Mercy in Mayville,

7. Sister M. Bernetta Quinn, "View from a Rock: The Fiction of Flannery O'Connor and J. F. Powers," *Critique,* II (Fall 1958), 24–25.

had given them a lecture on what to do if a young man should—here they laughed so hard they were not able to go on without going back to the beginning—on what to do if a young man should—they put their heads in their laps—on what to do if—they finally managed to shout it out—if he should "behave in an ungentlemanly manner with them in the back of an automobile." Sister Perpetua said they were to say, "Stop sir! I am a Temple of the Holy Ghost!" and that would put an end to it. The child sat up off the floor with a blank face. She didn't see anything so funny in this. What was really funny was the idea of Mr. Cheatam or Alonzo Myers beauing them around. That killed her (*Good Man,* p. 88) .

That these two girls are intended to be examples of those who remain ignorant of the sacraments through the triviality of their minds is demonstrated when Wendell and Cory Wilkins, twins who belong to the Church of God, visit them. The boys sit on the porch banister and sing "a hillbilly song that sounded half like a love song and half like a hymn" (p. 90) . Joanne and Susan mock the boys by singing *Tantum ergo Sacramentum,* a hymn from benediction. The little girl is incensed that the boys think "That must be Jew singing"; she does not perceive that their ignorance, arising from their lack of education, is less reprehensible than the girls' spiritual insensitivity.

Julian's mother in "Everything That Rises Must Converge," Thomas's mother in "The Comforts of Home," and Mary Grace's mother in "Revelation" do not express themselves directly concerning God or religion but clearly consider themselves to be right-thinking Christians. Their dominant trait is to mouth self-righteous moral platitudes. That all three are mothers constitutes, perhaps, a wry commentary on the conflict between generations apart from their more subtle relevance to religious themes. One should avoid an easy classification of them as generally unsympathetic, singly functional stereotypes. Although they perpetrate narrow and oversimplified attitudes toward life—attitudes which blind them to some basic truths—their charitable concern for their children and for others is genuine. Julian's mother, for example, offers a penny to the Negro child on the bus because she thinks it will bring some pleasure to him; although Julian in some respects is blinder than his mother, she does not see, as he does, that the child's mother will take her charitable gesture as an indication of condescension. Julian is right—condescension is truly part of her motivation; but his mother is unable to make such subtle distinctions. In similar fashion, she cannot understand Julian's resisting her attempts to identify him and herself with the defunct glories of their ancestors, the Chestnys and the Godhighs. Genealogical pride constitutes her rationale for arrogating herself; it is part of her general insensitivity in the matter of Christian charity and links her with many other characters in Flannery O'Connor's stories who believe in "good country people" with no discriminatory regard for the pitfalls inherent in such ethical oversimplification.

In "The Comforts of Home" Thomas's mother's blind charity moves her to befriend Sarah Ham, a criminally inclined nymphomaniac whose parole from jail she requests and assumes responsibility for. Sarah Ham is a thoroughly depraved person, and the mother's failure to acknowledge that condition is one measure of her

tragically shallow nature. When she reminds her outraged son that she would want someone to take him in
if he were in Sarah's predicament, her insight contains
sufficient truth to throw Thomas's own outrage into its
proper perspective: his belief in the virtue of modera-
tion is as much self-righteous rationalization as his
mother's generosity is poorly conceived good will. The
complementary nature of their respective attitudes
makes them a kind of unholy tweedledum and tweedle-
dee. Throughout the story the mother's observations
that Sarah (who calls herself Star Drake) looks like a
good girl and that she has been deprived of all the
comforts of home are contrasted to Thomas's exasper-
ated threats to leave home or to have the girl put back
in jail. While he is aware of his mother's good intentions, he contends, and with justification—for this is
one of the themes of the story—that she "make[s] a
mockery of virtue, to pursue it with such a mindless
intensity that everyone involved was made a fool of and
virtue itself became ridiculous."[8]

Mary Grace's mother in "Revelation" is not nearly so
important to the story as Julian's mother or Thomas's,
but she is like them in her tendency to offer easy solutions to extremely complex problems. Her problem is,
of course, Mary Grace, the ugly fat girl in the doctor's
office who attacks Mrs. Turpin, throwing at her a heavy
book on *Human Development,* calling her an "old wart
hog from hell," and attempting with great strength and
violence to choke her. The girl's mother is a "well-

8. Flannery O'Connor, *Everything That Rises Must Converge,*
p. 117. Further quotations from this work will be identified with
the abbreviation *Everything* and a page number in parentheses.

dressed greyhaired lady" whose first platitude has a cruel relevance to her daughter's condition—a meaning which the reader feels may very well not occur to her. The conversation has turned to fat people, and Mary Grace's mother remarks, "I don't think it makes a bit of difference what size you are. You just can't beat a good disposition" (*Everything*, p. 192). When Mrs. Turpin, the central figure of the story, observes that "There's a heap of things worse than a nigger," the woman responds with satisfaction in her voice, "Yes, and it takes all kinds to make the world go round" (pp. 200–201). That she does not have the charity nor the perception to apply her aphorism to her own daughter's situation is made obvious when she quite pointedly refers to her daughter's ill temper:

I think people with bad dispositions are more to be pitied than anyone on earth. . . . I think the worst thing in the world is an ungrateful person. To have everything and not appreciate it. I know a girl . . . who has parents who would give her anything, a little brother who loves her dearly, who is getting a good education, who wears the best clothes, but who can never say a kind word to anyone, who never smiles, who just criticizes and complains all day long (p. 205).

Again the phrase Thomas used about his mother—that she makes a mockery of virtue and destroys through her very good intentions—applies. Her mother's attempts to force Mary Grace to see her blessings and become the bland, sweet, and gregarious person that the mother believes herself to have been send the girl into a neurotic paroxysm of rage.

The characters discussed up to this point have been those who promote the religious themes of the stories

and novels in a negative sense, by illustrating corruption in order to throw its opposite into relief. If they do
not seem insistently to demonstrate a systematic concern with the sins subject to the exegesis of the church,
these characters do illustrate the failings most common
to ordinary fallen humanity. Insensitive to grace, they
are not so much evil as they are lukewarm, short-
sighted, and shallow.

An insensitivity to God's grace need not be accompanied by cynicism or satanic malice; in fact, some characters in Flannery O'Connor's stories are avowedly religious, quite firm in their belief, and yet clearly wrong;
in their error they are obviously as estranged from God
as those who make no pretense to know Him. Sarah
Ruth Cates Parker in "Parker's Back" and Mrs. Shortley in "The Displaced Person" are two of this type.

The central figure of "Parker's Back," Obadiah Eli-
hue Parker, is a loose-living, hard-cursing man whose
body, except for his back, is covered with tattoos. Following a religious experience in which God comes to
him in a burning tree ignited by the fuel from his
overturned tractor, he feels mysteriously compelled to
have the face of God tattooed on his back. The image
he chooses at the tattoo parlor is that of "the haloed
head of a flat stern Byzantine Christ with all-demanding eyes" (*Everything*, p. 235). After the image is com-
pleted, Parker defends it with his fists against the deri-
sion of his former friends in the pool parlor, and he
later realizes that "The eyes that were now forever on
his back were eyes to be obeyed" (p. 241). The irony of
Parker's obvious spiritual conversion is that Sarah
Ruth, his wife, has motivated him yet viciously rejects
the symbol of his new life when he shows it to her; she

considers the tattoo idolatry and beats Parker's back
until "large welts had formed on the face of the tattooed Christ" (p. 244). Caroline Gordon has pointed
out that this story represents dramatically the particular heresy that denies the corporeality of God,[9] which
may be deduced from Sarah Ruth's remark when shown
the face of God, "He don't *look* . . . He's a spirit. No
man shall see his face" (p. 244). Yet the reality of God's
face to Parker himself exists in his mind, for the image
is on his back and can therefore be seen by him only
indirectly through a mirror. The embodiment of Christ
in Parker is symbolized by the tattoo *on* him. In this
sense Sarah Ruth's religious wrongness is relevant to the
heresy indicated in Miss Gordon's remarks. The meaning of this heresy is broadened, however, by the satire of
Sarah Ruth's Bible Belt Protestantism, which directs
her religious attention against the outward forms of
religion at the expense of its moral and spiritual significance. Her religion is that of her father, "a Straight
Gospel preacher" (p. 229); in the name of it she is
"against color" and consequently against O. E.'s tattoos
inasmuch as they are "idolatrous, . . . no better than
what a fool Indian would do" (p. 225). Following the
same reasoning, she "thought churches were idolatrous," necessitating their marriage in the County Ordinary's office" (p. 229). Further, her religion emphasizes
prohibitions:

In addition to her other bad qualities, she was forever sniff-
ing up sin. She did not smoke or dip, drink whiskey, use bad

language or paint her face, and God knew some paint would have improved it, Parker thought. . . . Sometimes he supposed that she had married him because she meant to save him (p. 220).

Her procedure in saving O. E. would be to prevent him from doing the things he liked most, not to inspire him with the Holy Spirit. Her error, then, is that her espousal of a negative, prohibitive religion blinds her to the essential importance of a positive commitment to God. She does not realize that the image, the idol as she refers to it, on her husband's back represents to him a moral imperative, the inescapable, all-demanding eyes of Christ—as inescapable as "The ragged figure [Christ] which moves from tree to tree in the back of [Hazel Motes's] mind."[10]

Mrs. Shortley in "The Displaced Person" is as mistaken in her religious views, and as determined, as Sarah Ruth Cates Parker. She dominates Part I of the story and appears there as the "giant wife of the countryside" who gazes menacingly about but ignores the afternoon sun. Her ignoring of the sun foreshadows her ignorance of the nature of the true country, and her search for a sign of danger or trouble signals her misguided proud commitment to expose and rout Mr. Guizac, a European Roman Catholic, for his backward and dangerous notions. Robert Fitzgerald speaks of her as "an exponent of the countryside's religion,"[11] making her, like Sarah Ruth, subject to grotesque conceptions about religion, summed up in her vision of the day

10. Flannery O'Connor, "Author's Note to the Second Edition," *Wise Blood*, p. 5.
11. "The Countryside and the True Country," p. 385.

when the "ten million billion" displaced persons like Mr. Guizac take over:

She began to imagine a war of words, to see the Polish words and the English words coming at each other, stalking forward, not sentences, just words, gabble gabble gabble, flung out high and shrill and stalking forward and then grappling with each other. She saw the Polish words, dirty and all-knowing and unreformed, flinging mud on the clean English words until everything was equally dirty. She saw them all piled up in a room, all the dead dirty words, theirs and hers too, piled up like the naked bodies in the newsreel. God save me! she cried silently, from the stinking power of Satan! And she started from that day to read her Bible with new attention. She poured over the Apocalypse and began to quote from the Prophets and before long she had come to a deeper understanding of her existence. She saw plainly that the meaning of the world was a mystery that had been planned and she was not surprised to suspect that she had a special part in the plan because she was strong. She saw that the Lord God Almighty had created the strong people to do what had to be done and she felt that she would be ready when she was called (*Good Man,* p. 217) .

She identifies Mr. Guizac with the Roman Catholic priest who has placed him on Mrs. McIntyre's farm, and ascribes to both of them dark plots against the righteous. Her own calling to carry out some violence against them is, since both are clearly identified with the true country in which grace abounds, tantamount to crucifixion, throwing Mrs. Shortley into the role of false prophet and antichrist. But Mrs. Shortley's vehemence is empty and flabby, as her role as antichrist is ineffectual. She lives and dies pathetically, foolishly, and so participates in the dullness, insensitivity, and ignorance which characterize fools in general. Rayber's father, for example, is neither sympathetic with religion nor against it because he does not understand it. The spiritually blind characters, such as Julian's mother, have no notion of the sacramental view of life, and it is this ignorance that makes them blind in spiritual matters and insensitive to the opportunities for accepting grace. Similarly, Sarah Ruth Parker and Mrs. Shortley are incapable of transcending their narrow conceptions of religion; they profess to be Christians but have not the least understanding of the faith.

Unlike those O'Connor characters who are ignorant or insensitive to grace are those who represent various conscious, deliberate forms of disbelief, cynicism, and deception. One need not allegorize to define them as heathens, for in nearly every instance they are seen against a specifically—if sometimes outrageously—Christian background. The ironically named Mr. Paradise in "The River" is one of these. The central action of the story is the baptism of a child, Harry Ashfield, by a young faith healer, Bevel Summers, who is holding a meeting at the river, attracting the sick and the maimed. The cynicism of Mr. Paradise in regard to such miracles is indicated when Mrs. Connin, the babysitter who takes Harry to the river, says that Mr. Paradise, suffering from a cancer over his ear, "always comes [to healing] to show he ain't been healed" (*Good Man*, p. 37). At the healing he expresses his belief that Bevel Summers is more interested in the collection plate than in the health of the sick, and he guffaws with delight when Harry wants the preacher to pray for his mother, who is sick with a hangover. Furthermore, Mr. Paradise is specifically associated with pigs, which function throughout the story, as they do biblically, as symbols of spiritual uncleanliness. At Mrs. Connin's house Harry is traumatically frightened by pigs which trample him as they escape from the pen. Afterwards one of them comes to the house:

> The shoat climbed the two steps onto the back porch and stood outside the screen door, looking in with his head lowered sullenly. He was long-legged and hump-backed and part of one of his ears had been bitten off.
> "Git away!" Mrs. Connin shouted. "That one yonder favors Mr. Paradise that has the gas station," she said (p. 37).

Later in the story when Harry attempts to rebaptize himself, drowning as he embraces "the Kingdom of Christ in the river," he sees above him the vain and frantic attempts of Mr. Paradise to rescue him. Mr. Paradise appears to him "like a giant pig bounding after him, shaking a red and white club and shouting." Mr. Paradise is left "like some ancient water monster . . . empty-handed, staring with his dull eyes as far down the river line as he could see" (p. 52). He is a man unable to see the true country which Harry attained, and he is incredulous that one should seek it with the determination shown by Harry Ashfield.

Hoover Shoats in *Wise Blood,* whose name is not ironic but a direct indication of his nature, first appears as Onnie Jay Holy, appointing himself to the small crowd gathered at the entrance of a theater as Hazel Motes's first disciple. But he deliberately distorts Haze's doctrines of the Church Without Christ; while Haze's doctrine of truth through blasphemy results in a hard

inverse morality, difficult for hypocritical nonbelievers
to accept, Hoover Shoats offers them the chance to realize again the childlike sweetness inside them and to
achieve a smiling, joyful happiness that will ingratiate
them to their fellow men. He distorts the name of the
church envisioned by Haze, calling it the Holy Church
of Christ Without Christ, concluding his pitch with an
appeal for money: "It'll cost you each a dollar but what
is a dollar? A few dimes! Not too much to pay to unlock
that little rose of sweetness inside you!"[12] When Haze
denies him to the gathered crowd, declaring that he
"ain't true," Onnie Jay Holy tells him that they just
lost ten dollars, and reveals his total lack of religious
sincerity and his intent to pervert religion into a lucra-
tive business venture. He tells Haze that he is a real
preacher, having conducted a radio program called
"Soulease, a quarter hour of Mood, Melody, and Mentality," cautioning that one must "keep it sweet" if he
expects to "get anywhere in religion," and demeaning
Haze's concept of the "new jesus" by treating it as a
good business idea. When Haze explains to him that
"new jesus" is not a thing or a person "but a way to say
a thing" (*WB*, p. 159), Hoover dismisses him as an
"innerlekchul." Subsequently Shoats gets his revenge on
Hazel by finding Solace Layfield, outfitting him to look
and sound like Hazel, and drawing crowds to hear his
shadow of a false prophet. Hoover Shoats, then, unlike
Hazel, whose gross religious error is at least offered
from the standpoint of firm conviction, not only fails to
acknowledge religious truth, but damns himself further

12. Flannery O'Connor, *Wise Blood,* p. 153. Further quotations
from this work will be identified with the abbreviation *WB* and
a page number in parentheses.

by becoming a stumbling block for others and deform-
ing faith for no other purpose than his own selfish ends.

In the same novel, Asa Hawks, who poses as a blind
preacher, is a similar type. In his appeal to the people,
however, he makes no pretense, as Hoover Shoats does,
of giving them the sweet, innocuous message; instead he
deliberately mocks them and the religion that he
mouths, as if to declare that he deserves their help for
being as irreligious as they are. In him there is no
suggestion that he is driven to God and perverse prose-
lytizing through such backwoods, Bible Belt conviction
as can be seen in Bevel Summers in "The River" or old
Mason Tarwater in *The Violent Bear It Away,* or
Rufus Johnson in "The Lame Shall Enter First." When
Hawks tells Hazel Motes that Jesus loves him, he says it
in a "flat mocking voice" *(WB, p.* 53). He laughs when
he perceives Haze's tortured spiritual problems and
when he paraphrases the Bible. His ultimate and most
blasphemous mockery of religion is his feigned blindness, which he compares to that of Paul, whose story
had inspired Hawks ten years earlier "to blind himself
to justify his belief that Christ Jesus had redeemed
him" (p. 112). At the revival on the appointed night,
he had not the faith or nerve to make his promise good;
in his subsequent disillusionment, he blames Jesus for
his own cowardice and falls into surly bitterness. Although Hawks seems at that time to have been a perverse but sincere believer, his disillusionment (stem-
ming from his own cowardice and blamed by him on Jesus, who drove away the devils that possessed him) is
bitter and complete enough for him to refer to Haze as a
"Goddam Jesus-hog" (p. 109).

Whereas Asa Hawks represents cynicism and hypoc-

risy, his daughter Sabbath Lily is one of several straightforward heathens in Flannery O'Connor's works who
are obviously sinful and pursue their sinful ways without any conscience, without any sense of guilt. Because
they have never known innocence nor the hope of accepting grace, they are not disillusioned or cynical. Further, these heathens—Sabbath Lily Hawks, the parents
of Harry Ashfield in "The River," and Mrs. Leora Watts
in *Wise Blood*—do not resemble those who are invincibly ignorant and theologically wrong or those who lack
grace because of their complacency or self-righteousness; instead, they matter-of-factly enjoy the sinful life.
Sabbath Lily, like Edmund in *King Lear,* appears to be
relieved that as a bastard she need not concern herself
with achieving salvation. Her apparent preoccupation
with salvation when she is with' Haze has nothing to
do with a moral problem but is her way of letting Haze
know that she is amoral and physically available to
him. In her attempt to seduce him, she expresses her
sexual proposition as if it were a religious one: "I can
save you. . . . I got a church in my heart where Jesus is
King" (p. 121). When after several failures she succeeds in winning Hazel, she defines her heathenism
openly; referring to her reaction to him, she says,

That innocent look don't hide a thing, he's just pure filthy
right down to the guts, like me. The only difference is I like
being that way and he don't. Yes sir! . . . I like being that
way and I can teach you how to like it. Don't you want to
learn how to like it? (p. 169).

The final sign of her heathenism comes when she accepts the infant-sized mummy brought by Enoch Emery
(who takes it to be the "new jesus" that Haze has

preached about) as her own child, symbolizing the grotesque sterility of her sexual nature.

Equally sterile is the prostitute to whom Haze is
directed by a sign scribbled on the wall of a toilet at the
railroad station:

Mrs. Leora Watts!
60 Buckley Road
The friendliest bed in town!
Brother

Like Sabbath Lily, Mrs. Watts is the image of filth from
her first appearance to her final gesture of obscenity.
When Haze arrives at the address, he finds her on the
bed, cutting her toenails, a woman with yellow hair,
greasy white skin, small teeth "pointed and speckled
with green," clothed only in a pink nightgown. Although these features present the typically vulgar,
coarse prostitute that can be found throughout literature, Flannery O'Connor manages to make the religious
implications of this figure quite clear. Haze goes to the
woman "not for the sake of the pleasure in her, but to
prove that he didn't believe in sin since he practiced
what was called it" (p. 110). Even though he denies to
her that he is a preacher, she takes him to be one (as
did the taxi driver who drove Haze to her address) because of the stern, clerical black hat which he wears.
Haze was sexually innocent until his experience with
Mrs. Watts; it is her nature not only to delight in her
trade but to enhance her pleasure in it by defiling innocence. She multilates the symbol of Hazel Motes's basically devout soul—"After he was asleep, she had got up
and cut the top of his hat out in an obscene shape"
(p. 110).

The reader, then, is not allowed to overlook Mrs.
Watts's significance in the religious theme of the novel.
Indeed, the guilt which drives Hazel Motes both away
from God and toward Him throughout the novel is
specifically associated with an incident that Hazel remembers as he takes off his clothes that first night with
Mrs. Watts. He recalls attending at the age of ten a
carnival side show advertised as "SINsational": drawn
to it after his father has entered the tent, the boy imagines in his innocence that the sin has something to do
with a privy or that "they [are] doing something to a
nigger" (p. 61). What he sees when he finally gets past
the barker is

> something white . . . lying, squirming a little, in a box
> lined with black cloth. For a second he thought it was a
> skinned animal and then he saw it was a woman. She was
> fat and she had a face like an ordinary woman except there
> was a mole on the corner of her lip, that moved when she
> grinned, and one on her side (p. 62).

While watching, he hears his father say, "Had one of
themther build into ever' casket, . . . be a heap ready to
go sooner" (p. 62). This experience causes Haze first to
neglect the rest of the carnival, later to hide behind a
tree from the penetrating and knowing eyes of his
sternly religious mother, and finally to subject himself
to mortification by filling his shoes with stones and
small rocks and walking deliberately into the woods in
order to "satisfy Him" (pp. 63–64). The sight of the
woman in the coffin causes Haze's mortification, but
when his mother thrashes him subsequently for nothing
more than looking as if he has seen something evil, the
boy "forgot the guilt of the tent for the nameless un-

placed guilt that was in him" (p. 63) ; in Haze's mind, his loss of innocence ushers him into a world of sin that is general, pervasive, and not limited by the nature of the actual experience that triggered the recognition. Similarly, Mrs. Watts, a later embodiment of the woman in the coffin, represents not only the specific heathenism associated with the prostitute, but the generally corrupt condition of the world that signifies original sin, the fallen nature of man.

The Ashfield parents in "The River" also pursue heathenism as a way of life. Although they are created to provide a godless background for Harry, their child who is baptized, they constitute a detailed study in themselves. As the story opens on Sunday morning, they are sending Harry away for the day with a strange babysitter, Mrs. Connin. The mother is sick (Harry tells the preacher she has a hangover), spiritually as well as physically; not only is her child shabby and neglected, but he is deprived of love and is so accustomed to hearing such general profanity that he "thought Jesus Christ was a word like 'oh' or 'damn' or 'god,' or maybe somebody who had cheated them out of something sometime" (*Good Man*, p. 38) . Mrs. Connin cares for the child all day at her own home and takes him to a prayer healing at the river, where he is baptized. When Harry is returned to his parents, another party is in progress; those attending laughingly ridicule the prayer healing, Harry's baptism, and the book the child brings home, *The Life of Jesus Christ for Readers Under Twelve,* the only interest in it being shown by one man who thinks it is a collector's item because it was published in 1832. When his mother questions

Harry, she is concerned only about the "lies" he might have told about her. The dialogue between them twice describes her figuratively as on top of the river while the child is under it; the point is clear enough that the child, because of his baptism, participates in the river of life while his mother does not.

A parable sums up the destructiveness of the heathens' life of the flesh and divine retribution attendant upon it. Ironically, one of the heathens, Sabbath Lily Hawks, tells it:

Listen . . . , this here man and woman killed this little baby. It was her own child but it was ugly and she never give it any love. This child had Jesus and this woman didn't have nothing but good looks and a man she was living in sin with. She sent the child away and it come back and she sent it away again and it come back again and ever' time she sent it away, it come back to where she and this man was living in sin. They strangled it with a silk stocking and hung it up in the chimney. It didn't give her any peace after that, though. Everything she looked at was that child. Jesus made it beautiful to haunt her. She couldn't lie with that man without she saw it, staring through the chimney at her, shining through the brick in the middle of the night. . . . She didn't have nothing but good looks. . . . That ain't enough. No siree (*WB*, p. 52).

One can see then that such characters in Flannery O'Connor, like those in this parable, are not simply types of the dissolute, lustful, and gluttonous life. They are made specifically heathen so as to express the absence of Jesus Christ, the absence of grace, the loss of salvation in their lives because of their failure to acknowledge their sin and bewail it; what is true of those who are ignorant and foolish is even more applicable to the heathens—they have undergone no revelation that would lead them to rising and ultimately toward convergence.

The various forms of spiritual deficiency examined up to this point have revealed either a failure in understanding Christianity (the ignorant, the spiritually blind, and the misled fanatics) or an open, flagrant rejection of it for transitory personal reasons (the cynical, weak deceivers and the willful heathens). Unlike either of these major categories is that which includes two closely related groups, both of them made up of characters who reject Christianity not on insubstantial personal grounds, but on the basis of extended or concentrated philosophical consideration. The first group in this category includes atheists who have rejected Christianity in favor of some secular doctrine to which they are strongly devoted; the second includes characters who have examined Christianity critically in the light of their experience, found it inadequate, and consequently rejected the possibility of meaning in life or spun meanings out of themselves.

The atheists are of several types: those who reject Christianity as a dangerous myth which interferes with the psychological and social adjustment of the individual—Rayber in *The Violent Bear It Away* and Sheppard in "The Lame Shall Enter First"; those who reject Christianity on the basis of existentialist philosophical positions that lead them to belief only in nothingness— Hulga Hopewell in "Good Country People," and Hazel Motes in the early chapters of *Wise Blood;* and those who reject Christianity because of a proud belief in their capability to find a new jesus compatible with their own needs—Enoch Emery in *Wise Blood.*

Just as Asa Hawks is a kind of inverse "spiritual father" to Hazel Motes in *Wise Blood;*[13] George Rayber, the psychology teacher in *The Violent Bear It Away,* is both antagonist and hero to Francis Marion Tarwater, his nephew, who goes to Rayber's home after old Mason Tarwater dies. The nephew is attracted to Rayber because of his atheism, his rejection of the old man's violent religious belief, which has placed an unwanted responsibility upon the fourteen-year-old Tarwater; at the same time the boy hates the psychologist because the man cannot act decisively and because he represents a serious threat to the fulfillment of the mission prophesied for the boy by his great-uncle. This mission is twofold: the boy's first mission is to baptize Bishop Rayber, the idiot child of the teacher; his general mission is to "Go warn the children of God . . . of the terrible speed of justice" (*Violent,* p. 60) . The same responsibility would have been Rayber's except for circumstances; as a child, Rayber himself had been kidnapped by Mason Tarwater, baptized, and infected with religious zeal during four days at Powderhead before his godless parents took him home; once after that, Rayber tried to return to Powderhead, but at fourteen he had become bitterly disillusioned at the failure of the old man's prophecies, returning to him then only to mock and curse his uncle and everything he stood for. Sumner J. Ferris points out that Rayber, at the age of

13. Jonathan Baumbach. *The Landscape of Nightmare,* p. 90.

confirmation, has willingly chosen "the condition of the Pharisee . . . , the way of rationalism."[14] As an adult responsible for his sister's child, Rayber declares that the young Tarwater (later kidnapped by Mason and taken to Powderhead) will be "brought up to live in the real world. He's going to be brought up to expect exactly what he can do for himself. He's going to be his own saviour" (p. 70).

Because the seed of Christian belief planted in him by the old man remains even though it has fallen on barren ground, Rayber must "devote his life to keeping it from growing; that is, to maintaining his rational equilibrium and rejecting grace."[15] At one point he goes to the extreme of blasphemy by rebaptizing Tarwater before his uncle's eyes; moments after Mason has baptized his grandnephew, Rayber pours the remaining water over the child's buttocks and repeats the words of baptism. At most other times, however, Rayber proudly controls his emotions; the lifeless and mechanistic quality of his rationalism is symbolized by his hearing aid, which allows him to silence the word of God—actually and symbolically. At a tabernacle he frantically tries to shut the device off when a child evangelist points to him accusingly: "I see a damned soul before my eye! I see a dead man Jesus hasn't raised. His head is in the window but his ear is deaf to the Holy Word!" (*Violent*, p. 134). Symbolically, the hearing aid represents Rayber's attempt to transfer the center of his understanding from his heart of his head; Tarwater asks him, "Do you think

14. "The Outside and the Inside: Flannery O'Connor's *The Violent Bear It Away*," *Critique*, III (Winter-Spring 1960), 15.
15. *Ibid.*, pp. 15–16.

in the box . . . , or do you think in your head?" (p.
105). Knowing that the zealous Tarwater blood rages
in him and drives him towards God, Rayber becomes
deliberately an unholy, secular saint, controlling his
violent blood "by what amounted to a rigid ascetic
discipline" (p. 114), sleeping in a narrow bed, eating
frugally, and believing devotedly in his choice of emptiness rather than madness.

In the name of secular truth, Rayber instructs Tarwater that the dead do not rise again and even offers to
allow him to baptize Bishop to prove that baptism is no
more than an empty act. The depth of his opposition to
the Christian, sacramental view of life is shown in his
response to the preaching of the child evangelist at the
tabernacle, whose subject is the divine deliverance of
Christ from Herod's edict. Rayber sees the slaughtered
children as images of children slain not by Herod but
by the Lord; as the child preaches, Rayber imagines
that his mission is to "gather all the exploited children
of the world and let the sunshine flood their minds" (p.
133). From the Christian's point of view this incident
illustrates two important errors in Rayber's understanding of the world. First, he believes that Jesus was no
more than another child whose existence is no more nor
no less important than any one of the slaughtered inno-
cents; his failure to understand the justness of the sacrifice of the children for Christ indicates his complete
lack of sympathy with the Christian scheme of redemption, that One has laid down his life so that others may
live. Rayber's analysis is a complete inversion of the
Christian scheme of redemption in that he would have
Christ die in a totally secular context to save the mortal,

secular lives of the world. His second error is similar to the first: it is his failure to solve the problem of evil from a Christian point of view; in his sociological, secular context, the poor, the lame, the feeble-minded (such as his own son Bishop, who signifies to him "the general hideousness of fate" [p. 113]) are no more than accidents of nature, relating neither to the ravages of original sin nor to the need for purification; the salvation he envisions will be effected, not by baptism or spiritual ministry, but by medical and social rehabilitation.

Ironically, Rayber's only love, other than a vague social benevolence, is the "hated love" which he feels for Bishop. Strangely drawn to the child, Rayber separates from his wife when she wants to place her child in an institution. In providing a focal point for Rayber's love and for his need to suffer for others outside the framework of Christianity, Bishop becomes for him a substitute for Christ. Rayber realizes "that his own stability depended on the little boy's presence" (p. 182), and that without him his general urge to a "terrifying love" would, to his horror, become directed to the whole world. Rayber fears the time when the world "would become his idiot child," bringing him to the necessity of anesthetizing his life rather than submit to such a fanatical extreme. He suppresses his fears, but they return as persistently as does Tarwater's urge to baptize Bishop: "[Rayber] felt a sinister pull on his consciousness, the familiar undertow of expectation, as if he were still a child waiting on Christ" (p. 182). Rayber rationally manipulates even his very real and urgent love so that it has no resemblance to Christian charity; when his heart responds to the first sight of

Tarwater, it pounds "like the works of a gigantic machine in his chest" (p. 106), and Rayber identifies, not with the boy's fear and loneliness, but with his blasphemy and disrespect for his great-uncle.

Old Mason Tarwater's analysis of his nephew—"He's full of nothing" (p. 56)—is borne out throughout the novel by Rayber's lack of violence and decisiveness, and by his mechanical response to the world. Near the end of the novel, aware of defeat by Tarwater and of the imminent loss of Bishop, Rayber is "indifferent to his own dissolution" and relishes the idea that "To feel nothing [is] peace" (p. 200). In his room at the Cherokee Lodge, when he becomes mysteriously aware that Tarwater is drowning Bishop, "he grabbed the metal box of the hearing aid as if he were clawing his heart," and as the child bellows, "The machine made the sounds seem to come from inside him as if something in him were tearing itself free" (p. 202). Knowing that Bishop is dying, he is certain only that he must remain in control of himself, "that no cry must escape him." Ironically, however, he no longer needs to exorcise his urges to charity and pity, for at the death of his son his own dehumanization descends upon him like damnation itself, like the terrible speed of God's justice prophesied by his uncle:

He stood waiting for the raging pain, the intolerable hurt that was his due, to begin, so that he could ignore it, but he continued to feel nothing. He stood light-headed at the window and it was not until he realized there would be no pain that he collapsed (p. 203).

Ferris explains that Rayber exemplifies one meaning

of the epigraph of the novel: "From the days of John the Baptist until now, the kingdom of Heaven suffereth violence, and the violent bear it away." One of the meanings of this passage as Catholic exegetes understand it applies to Tarwater: the faithful shall attain the kingdom of heaven. The other applies to Rayber: "that the Pharisees, despite John's prophecy and Christ's ministry, still remain unbelievers and try to deny the faithful their reward."[16]

Sheppard, the city recreation director in "The Lame Shall Enter First," also illustrates the same meaning of the epigraph. This story, involving Sheppard, his son Norton, and Rufus Johnson, a lame boy taken charitably out of a reformatory, is a clear reworking of the Rayber-Bishop-Tarwater relationship. Mechanical and rational like Rayber, Sheppard urges Rufus Johnson (who is as infected with God as Tarwater is) to save himself and attempts to "enlighten" him through books, telescopes, and a civic education; to rehabilitate him with new clothes, a good home life, and an orthopedically designed shoe to correct his club foot. While Rufus betrays and mocks him, Sheppard continues to ignore the needs of his own child. Norton mourns constantly and pathetically for his dead mother, and he eagerly listens to Rufus Johnson's highly dramatic explanations of heaven, hell, and life after death. Norton desperately believes Rufus's contention that the boy will be united with his mother at his own death; as a result of Rufus's teaching and Sheppard's neglect,

16. *Ibid.,* p. 15.

Norton hangs himself in the attic. Unlike Rayber, Sheppard undergoes a revelation and suffers grief as he contemplates Norton's suicide and his own emptiness:

His heart constricted with a repulsion for himself so clear and intense that he gasped for breath. He had stuffed his own emptiness with good works like a glutton. He had ignored his own child to feed his vision of himself. He saw the clear-eyed Devil, the sounder of hearts, leering at him from the eyes of Johnson (*Everything*, p. 190).

Hulga Hopewell, the central figure in "Good Country People," is spoken of by one critic as "another of Flannery O'Connor's obdurate neo-pagans."[17] Although she and Hazel Motes are not characters who fail to achieve grace through recognition and acknowledgement of their errors, both of them demonstrate an important kind of spiritual corruption similar to that of Rayber, Sheppard, and Enoch Emery. Brainard Cheney has referred to this particular corruption in speaking of *Wise Blood* as a "bitter parody [of] atheistic existentialism."[18] In the fashion of the existentialist, Hazel Motes claims, "I don't have to run from anything because I don't believe in anything." The meaninglessness and the nothingness of the universe are the central doctrine of his belief:

I preach there are all kinds of truth, your truth and somebody else's but behind all of them, there's only one truth and that is that there's no truth. . . . No truth behind all

17. Rainulf Stelzmann, "Shock and Orthodoxy: An Interpretation of Flannery O'Connor's Novels and Short Stories," *Xavier University Studies*, II (March 1963), 10.

18. "Flannery O'Connor's Campaign for Her Country," *Sewanee Review*, LXXII (Autumn 1964), 556.

truths is what I and this church preach! Where you come from is gone, where you thought you were going to never was there, and where you are is no good unless you can get away from it. Where is there a place for you to be? No place.

Nothing outside you can give you any place. . . . You needn't to look at the sky because it's not going to open up and show no place behind it. You needn't to search for any hole in the ground to look through into somewhere else. You can't go neither forwards nor backwards into your daddy's time nor your children's if you have them. In yourself right now is all the place you've got. If there was any Fall, look there, if there was any Redemption, look there, and if you expect any Judgment, look there, because they all three will have to be in your time and your body and where in your time and your body can they be? (*WB,* p. 165–166) .

The same conclusions have been drawn by Hulga Hopewell, whose Ph.D. in philosophy lends ironic sanction to her beliefs. She tells the Bible salesman, Manley Pointer, that she has seen '*through* to nothing," and that seeing nothing in this fashion is "a kind of salvation" (*Good Man,* p. 191) . The fact that she has lost one of her legs and wears an artificial one symbolizes her spiritual incompleteness, and her willful devotion to error shows in her eyes, which have "the look of someone who has achieved blindness by an act of will and means to keep it" (*Good Man,* p. 171) .

The existentialist's dilemma—Kierkegaard's Christian Either/Or and Sartre's atheistic Being or Nothingness—is a theme often encountered in Flannery O'Connor's fiction. Hulga, Hazel Motes, and Tarwater all struggle violently to believe in nothing, to renounce the insistent religious orientation passed on to them by a father or a father-substitute. And the choice available to them is an extreme and narrow one; they do not interpret their choice as one between vague religious belief and solid secular values based on reason, but as a choice between an all-consuming evangelical commitment to God and nothingness—the complete repudiation of *any* values at all. Although Hulga does not appear to be as tormented by choice as Tarwater and Hazel Motes, implicitly she is as torn by doubt as they are. When she surrenders her artificial leg to the Bible salesman (whom she associates with "good country people" of strong religious faith, but who turns out to be a hardened, cynical believer in nothingness), she is affirming faith in him; she is risking and hazarding everything for the sake of love. When he betrays her with smutty playing cards, whiskey, and a package of contraceptives taken from a hollowed-out Bible, she is shocked into asking the very question which previously aroused her scorn for her mother, whose illusions remain intact: "Aren't you just good country people?" (p. 194). Hulga, then, like the others, is finally demonstrated as incapable of belief in nothingness; unlike them, she is also incapable of the total commitment to the opposite of nothingness. She embodies the weakness of modern man who cannot believe in nothing yet is equally unable to profess with assurance a belief in anything. Like Rayber after the death of Bishop, who can feel neither pleasure nor pain, salvation nor the tortures of damnation, modern man is pathetic. Further pathos in this form of neo-paganism lies in the fact that when some substitute for belief arises (in this story, Hulga's resolve to seduce the Bible salesman, in her mind an action which will lend concrete reality to her theoretical belief in nothing), its insufficiency or outright evil deceptiveness as a solution to a spiritual problem is manifest.

The Misfit, the pathological killer who murders an entire family in "A Good Man is Hard to Find," is, as Robert McCown puts it, "a soul blasted by the sin of despair."[19] In Kierkegaard, despair is the sickness unto death experienced by those separated from God and overcome by those who through the leap of faith to God find being again. In Sartre, despair is the nausea that accompanies the realization that one is no more than a *thing*. The Misfit has resolved his despair into a belief in nothingness, not by a leap of faith. It is because he has ceased to believe in anything that he is able to murder the entire family without the slightest remorse. This crime is the gratuitous act of the existentialist, carried out to demonstrate the meaninglessness of the world. Significantly, in the Freudian terms of the prison psychiatrist, the Misfit's crimes represent the murder of his father—which he claims he knew "for a lie" (*Good Man*, p. 26). Symbolically, this crime is the murder of God, after which despair descends, to be followed by one meaningless act after another, crimes leading only to the dead end the Misfit found at the conclusion of the story: "'Shut up, Bobby Lee,' the Misfit said. 'It's no real pleasure in life'" (p. 29).

Just as Rayber takes the deformity of his child as an indication of the absence of God, so is the Misfit unable to understand the problem of evil. "I call myself The Misfit," he says, "because I can't make what all I done

19. "Flannery O'Connor and the Reality of Sin," *Catholic World*, CLXXXVIII (January 1959), 289.

wrong fit what all I gone through in punishment" (p. 28). His statement is no doubt true, but it applies equally well to Christ when He was crucified, and to man in general in a fallen world in which evil seems to overwhelm him for no reason. Christ and Christians, however, know that good and evil do not balance out in the manner expected by the Misfit.

Enoch Emery in *Wise Blood* is the most fully developed of the neo-pagans who fail to achieve an epiphany that indicates their acceptance of grace. Since he functions in the novel as a foil for Hazel Motes, it is not surprising that in him too can be seen the characteristics of the existentialist. The most persistent feature of his portrait is the isolation, alienation, or separateness typical of the existentialist's explanation of man's condition. Enoch has been compelled by his father to move to Taulkinham, where he works for the city as a park attendant. Though he professes to be proud of his job and to like the city, time after time he complains to Hazel Motes that he knows no one, and in one scene after another he attempts to ingratiate himself to waitresses, street hawkers, strangers on the street (such as Haze, who rejects his offer of friendship), and finally with Gonga, a surly man in a gorilla suit who tells Enoch to go to hell as Enoch shakes his hand outside the movie theater. His isolation is aggravated further by his chaotic family background; he tells Haze that "Thisyer woman that traded me from my daddy . . . was a Welfare woman" (*WB*, p. 44).

Enoch reveres this father whom the welfare department considered an unfit parent: "My daddy looks just like Jesus. . . . His hair hangs to his shoulders. Only difference is he's got a scar acrost his chin. I ain't never seen who my mother is" (p. 51) . His father's wise blood gives the novel its title; even though Enoch claims to "know a whole heap about Jesus," it is his father's wisdom, not Christ's, that he turns to for direction. This belief in one's own blood, in his own identity as the ultimate measure of truth, is at the very heart of existentialist doctrine; as Sartre explains:

Atheistic existentialism, which I represent, is more coherent. It states that if God does not exist, there is at least one being in whom existence precedes essence, a being who exists before he can be defined by any concept, and that this being is man. . . . Not only is man what he conceives himself to be, but he is also only what he wills himself to be after this thrust toward existence.

But if existence really does precede essence, man is responsible for what he is. Thus, existentialism's first move is to make every man aware of what he is and to make the full responsibility of his existence rest on him.

Man makes himself. He isn't ready made at the start. In choosing his ethics, he makes himself.[20]

Enoch seeks his salvation through his own blood and that of his father, not through the redeeming blood of Jesus Christ. In contrast to Haze, Enoch is the fully realized existentialist; whereas Haze is devoted only to nothingness (he tells Hoover Shoats that the new jesus is only a way of saying something, that something being nothingness) , Enoch Emery has made what Sartre refers to as the "thrust toward existence" by focusing his life upon a literal new jesus and making a religion of it even before he has heard Haze preach.

20. Jean-Paul Sartre, *Existentialism*, pp. 18, 19, 51.

His neo-paganistic religion is fashioned by him around a "mystery" in "the dark secret center of the park" (p. 82) where he works; the mystery is a shrunken man in a glass case: "He was about three feet long. He was naked and a dried yellow color and his eyes were drawn almost shut as if a giant block of steel were falling down on top of him" (p. 98). Enoch tells Haze that the notice describing the mummy "says he was once as tall as you or me. Some A-rabs did it to him in six months" (p. 98). The place in which this figure rests is the MVSEVM, the religious significance of which is indicated by Enoch's fear of pronouncing the word. Every day he visits the shrine of his religion, carrying out a rigid order of worship, the steps of which might be taken to correspond to the successive stages of the Mass or the stations of the cross. The first of these is at the swimming pool, where Enoch hides in the abelia bushes and watches the women in bathing suits; when one woman pulls the bathing suit straps off her shoulders, Enoch whispers, "King Jesus." His voyeurism represents the extent to which pagan indulgence of the appetite is a sterile substitution for the spiritual activity of man when he identifies his existence with God. The next stage of his ritual takes place in the "FROSTY BOTTLE, a hotdog stand in the shape of an Orange Crush with frost painted in blue around the top of it" (p. 82), where his partaking of a chocolate malted milkshake is the grotesque pagan equivalent of the sacrificial wine in Holy Communion (a perversion which Hazel Motes significantly does not participate in); its sordidness is enhanced by the lewd remarks made by Enoch to the waitress, a vulgar priestess who refers to Enoch as "that

pus-marked bastard zlurping through that straw . . . ,
a goddamned son a bitch" (p. 91). Unmoved by this
vilification, Enoch proceeds along his unholy way to the
animal cages where he spits upon the wolves, which he
calls hyenas, and utters obscenities before the cages of
other animals, his hatred of them arising partly from
his envy of the care and feeding administered to them
by the attendants. Although one of the cages that seems
to be empty is of no interest to Enoch, Hazel stands
before it as if it were the empty tomb of the risen Christ,
and when he realizes that it is occupied by an owl with
one eye open, the eye becomes the gaze of God, to which
he protests, as he had earlier to the waitress, "I AM
clean" (p. 95).

Finally at the MVSEVM, Enoch ascends the ritually
numbered ten steps to the porch, ushers in his unwilling
novice, explains the mystery to him in "a church whis-
per," and resents the intrusion of a mother and her
children as that of the uninitiated. He is undeterred in
his mission to bring the new jesus to his new friend,
even though Hazel abandons him in the museum and
knocks him unconscious with a rock as he attempts to
follow. After this experience, he begins an ascetic discipline in which unaccountably to himself, he saves
money (partially by stealing some of his frugal needs),
fasts, and improves the condition of his rented bedroom. The most important piece of furniture in this
room is "a tabernacle-like cabinet which was meant to
contain a slop-jar" (p. 131). On one level this wash-
stand symbolizes Enoch's solipsism, for its ornate exte-
rior is climaxed by an oval mirror and Enoch "had
dreamed of unlocking the cabinet and getting in it and

then proceeding to certain rites and mysteries that he had a very vague idea about in the morning" (p. 132). This image of Enoch in the cabinet prefigures the ultimate purpose of the cabinet as a tabernacle for the shrunken man; Enoch, in other words, has found a god in the image of himself, mummified and unresurrected. Realizing that his wise blood has led him to create a place for his idol, he understands too that he has found the new Jesus that Hazel Motes has been preaching about.

When Enoch steals the shrunken man from the museum (his actual lack of true identity being symbolized here in his disguse as a Negro) and presents it to the one whom he considers the prophet of his neo-paganism, Hazel, as Jonathan Baumbach says, "recognizes it as himself—his double," and destroys it in an act of self-murder. Enoch Emery, on the other hand, continues his spiritual descent, affirming his identity with the animals at the zoo by grotesquely incarnating himself in the gorilla costume worn by the man at the theater, whom he murders. Baumbach explains that Enoch's imbruting himself constitutes a reversal of the evolutionary process and is an absurd, grotesque redemption.[21] The futility of attempts such as Enoch's to find salvation in a new dispensation, a new jesus, is insisted upon by Flannery O'Connor in her unmistakable rounding off of his function in the novel. Having fully assumed his new identity in the gorilla suit, Enoch practices growling, beating his chest, and extending his paw in friendship as Gonga had done to the children at the theater. Finding an actual man and woman to befriend, he offers his

21. *Op. cit.*, p. 91.

hand. They flee in terror, taking him for the brute that he is, not at his own estimate of himself. He is left there staring over the valley and the skyline of the city; after his character reaches its culmination in the epitome of bestiality, isolation, and spiritual emptiness, Enoch's story is over, his life determined, and his role in the novel ended.

All of O'Connor's neo-pagans do not end pathetically as Enoch and Rayber do, nor with terrifying decisiveness and action as the Misfit does. Those who, like Hulga and Sheppard, arrive at an epiphany after their fine logic fails suffer the agony attendant upon profound disillusionment. All share an intense devotion to their common sophistry.

In spite of all the error, corruption, and malice apparent in the bulk of Flannery O'Connor's characters, her people are for the most part representatives of fallen mankind, never worthy but always subject to grace and eligible for redemption. Only a few characters are more deeply evil, and they incarnate the force and living presence of a chaotic, destructive, and dark principle of evil in the world; these characters are agents of, or physical embodiments of, the devil. Flannery O'Connor believed very strongly in such an active principle of evil; in one of her letters she complains bitterly of two deficiencies in the majority of her audience: they no longer believe in the validity of the sacraments, and they do not know the devil.[22] As a writer she admit-

22. Letter from Flannery O'Connor to Andrew Lytle, February 4, 1960, Tennessee State Library and Archives, Nashville, Tennessee.

tedly incorporates the devil in her stories and novels and
hopes that he will be readily recognizable: "I want to be
certain that the devil gets identified as the devil and not
simply taken for this or that psychological tendency."[23]
In a highly provocative article, "Flannery O'Connor's
Devil," John Hawkes argues that she herself as a writer
reveals a Hawthornesque black authorial stance which
paradoxically permits her to sympathize with both the
satanic analysis of man and his victimization by the
devil:

My own feeling is that just as the creative process threatens
the Holy throughout Flannery O'Connor's fiction by gener-
ating a paradoxical fusion of improbability and passion out
of the Protestant "do-it-yourself" evangelism of the South,
and thereby raises the pitch of apocalyptic experience when
it finally appears; so too, throughout this fiction, the creative process transforms the writer's objective Catholic
knowledge of the devil into an authorial attitude in itself in
some measure diabolical. This is to say that in Flannery
O'Connor's most familiar stories and novels the "disbelief
. . . that we breathe in with the air of the times" emerges
fully as two-sided or complex as "attraction for the Holy."[24]

Brainard Cheney labels this article "a *tour de force*
remarkable only for foolhardiness,"[25] contending in re-
buttal that the religious themes of this fiction necessi-
tate convincing treatment of their opposites: "This
disbelief is party to our central religious conflict of the
day. And I might add that it constitutes a strategic

23. Quoted by John Hawkes, "Flannery O'Connor's Devil,"
Sewanee Review, LXX (Summer 1962) , 400.
24. *Ibid.*, pp. 400–401.
25. "Miss O'Connor Creates Unusual Humor Out of Ordinary
Sin," *Sewanee Review*, LXXI (Autumn 1963) , 646.

circumstance of Miss O'Connor's drama and satire."[26] Indeed, it would be most unlike Flannery O'Connor to create a weak, unconvincing straw man; writing to a novice writer seeking her advice, she insistently demands that the writer *see* and describe his characters with the greatest of accuracy and that he not "go into the heads of people you don't know anything about and have them think with your words and not their own."[27] Thus to characterize the devil (traditionally an attractive and convincing role) is to risk the sort of misunderstanding apparent in "Flannery O'Connor's Devil," but she was a writer who did not compromise her art by avoiding its risks. Just as Milton's Satan may be mistakenly taken as a heroic figure if one fails to trace his character to its ultimate degeneration, so might Flannery O'Connor's devils be misinterpreted when considered out of their thematic context.

Not all of the characters in this category are unilaterally satanic. For example, Powell Boyd and his companions from Atlanta who harass Mrs. Cope in "A Circle in the Fire" are in one sense the victims of the woman's self-righteousness. Once they are motivated by her selfishness, however, they become devilish agents of destruction and malice. They come from the city—often associated in Flannery O'Connor's fiction with the godless, the damned, and the dispossessed—to the country, a paradise from which Powell discovers he has been irrevocably cast out. Like Satan in *Paradise Lost* viewing Eden as a creation as magnificient as that which he

26. *Ibid.,* p. 649.
27. Sister Mary Alice, O. P., "My Mentor, Flannery O'Connor," *Saturday Review,* May 29, 1965, p. 24.

has lost, the boys are moved to "pale ire and envy."
When first rebuffed, they simply refuse to acknowledge
that they have no claim to Mrs. Cope's farm, proceeding
to ride the horses and make whatever use of the place
they wish without her permission. Upon further admo-
nition from her, they resort to ruthless destruction. Finally, their despair leads them to a position comparable
to Satan's when, recognizing the impossibility of regain-
ing paradise, he decides that those who possess it must
lose it, declaring, "Evil, be thou my good." The boys'
laughs as they go about their destructive business are
"vicious," and "full of calculated meanness" (*Good
Man*, p. 149). Deciding upon a course of action appropriate to the frustration they feel, they reason: "If this
place was not here any more . . . , you would never
have to think of it again" (p. 152). Their modern
diabolism first conceives the impractical but appropriate punishment of covering this Eden with a vestige of
their own objective hell, a parking lot. The more traditionally symbolic expedient they decide upon is fire;
they ignite the woods, shrieking as the flames grow.
That these boys are pathetic and that they function as
did Shadrach, Meshach, and Abednego in no way indicates that they are sympathetic characters; their function as agents of God depends on the orthodox Christian
belief that the actions of Satan are permitted by God
for the furtherance of his glory. Flannery O'Connor
assumes this when she says, "I suppose the devil teaches
most of the lessons that lead to self-knowledge."[28] In "A
Circle in the Fire," however, Mrs. Cope fails to learn.

28. Quoted by Hawkes, p. 406.

The powers of evil in "A View of the Woods" express themselves through the progress fiercely anticipated by old Mark Fortune, the grandfather of Mary Fortune Pitts. The simple rural purity of his farm, associated with the symbolic meaning of the true country, is of no consequence to him, and he wishes to "improve" it with paved roads, supermarkets, fish camps, gasoline stations, and "drive-in picture-shows," all such progress culminating in his vision of a town to be called Fortune in honor of him. On the other hand, his daughter's family, The Pittses, whom he allows to live on the land but not to buy it from him, cherish the place as it is, particularly the view of the woods which will be destroyed when Mr. Fortune sells the "lawn" to a businessman named Tilman as a site for a gas station. Tilman is the satanic figure under whose spell old Fortune operates; he conducts his business from a pandemonium "bordered on either side by a field of old used-car bodies . . . , outdoor ornaments, such as stone cranes and chickens, urns, jardinieres, whirligigs, and further back from the road, so as not to depress his dance-hall customers, a line of tombstones and monuments" (*Everything*, p. 67). The general appearance of Tilman at the signing of the bill of sale is so serpentine that one cannot ignore the implication. The agreement with Satan precipitates the action that leads swiftly to Mark Fortune's violent death. Having crushed his granddaughter's skull on a rock to protect himself from her attack upon him and to teach her a lesson of obedience to him whom she has defied for his sale of the lawn, Mr. Fortune, in the throes of a fatal heart attack, staggers without success to reach the water; as he does, a bulldozer excavating for a new fish camp is transformed into an image of the damnation to which he is delivered:

He looked around desperately for someone to help him but the place was deserted except for one huge yellow monster which sat to the side, as stationary as he was, gorging itself on clay (p. 81).

The embodiment of the devil in "Good Country People," Manley Pointer, the nineteen-year-old Bible salesman who uses a different name at every house he visits and who claims at the end of the story to have believed in nothing since he was born, serves to teach a lesson in self-knowledge to Hulga Hopewell, his betrayal of her revealing the futility of her own belief in nothingness by cruelly objectifying its destructive effect upon human needs for love. But he is also the devourer of souls alluded to in I Peter 5:8: "Be sober, be vigilant; because your adversary the devil, as a roaring lion, walketh about, seeking whom he may devour." Although one would not expect Mrs. Hopewell to take Manley Pointer as anything but "good country people," "the salt of the earth," it is highly ironical that Hulga, who takes pride in exposing sham and hypocrisy, should fail to recognize the adversary. "We are all damned," (*Good Man*, p. 191) she tells him condescendingly, little realizing that the drama of the loss of her own soul to the devil has already begun; the Bible salesman has slipped her glasses into his pocket, and when she next looks at the countryside, "She didn't realize he had taken her glasses but this landscape could not seem exceptional to her for she seldom paid any close attention to her surroundings" (p. 190). That her soul is being bargained for is made even clearer when Manley Pointer asks that Hulga show him "where your wooden leg joins on":

But she was as sensitive about the artificial leg as a peacock about his tail. No one ever touched it but her. She took care of it as someone else would his soul, in private and almost with her own eyes turned away (p. 192).

When she relinquishes her leg to him, she "felt entirely dependent on him. Her brain seemed to have stopped thinking altogether and to be about some other function that it was not very good at" (p. 193). She has been robbed of her entire self: her intellectuality, her body, and her soul. The Bible salesman reveals fully his satanic nature as he leaves, declaring his belief in nothing, packing up Hulga's leg in his valise, and gloating over other such conquests, in one of which he "got a woman's glass eye."

By far the most extensive use of the satanic character appears in *The Violent Bear It Away,* in which the devil assumes a role quite similar to that of the bad angel in a medieval morality play, appearing throughout the novel to offer evil counsel to Tarwater in hopes of claiming his soul. Like his medieval counterpart, this devil gains a hearing through Tarwater's own weakness, for when he is first heard after old Mason Tarwater's death, it is in the boy's own words of impatience at having to bury his great-uncle: "The voice sounded like a stranger's voice, as if the death had changed him instead of his great-uncle" (*Violent,* p. 11). To Tarwater the voice is at first objectionable, identified as "the stranger," but it is soon familiar enough to him to acknowledge at times as his other self and as a friend, becoming at the height of his influence "his faithful friend, lean, shadow-like, who had counseled him in both country and city" (p. 214). It was this devil and his later manifestation in the flesh that old Mason Tarwater warned his nephew against:

"You are the kind of boy," the old man said, "that the devil is always going to be offering to assist, to give you a smoke or a drink or a ride, and to ask you your bidnis. You had better mind how you take up with strangers. And keep your bidnis to yourself." It was to foil the devil's plans for him that the Lord had seen to his upbringing (p. 58).

Tarwater's "bidnis" is to baptize Bishop Rayber and to prophesy the terrible speed of God's mercy, and it is this mission which the devil seeks to prevent. He tells Tarwater that his choice is not between Jesus or the devil, as the boy asserts, but between "Jesus or *you*" (p. 39). As for the devil's analysis of Jesus and redemption, it is in essence that of Rayber, whose counsel to his nephew frequently echoes that of the voice, especially when it offers insidiously rational arguments:

Well now, the stranger said, don't you think any cross you set up in the year 1952 would be rotted out by the year the Day of Judgment comes in? Rotted to as much dust as his ashes if you reduced him to ashes? And lemme ast you this: what's God going to do with sailors drowned at sea that the fish have et and the fish that et them et by other fish and they et by yet others? And what about people that get burned up naturally in house fires? Burnt up one way or an other or lost in machines until they're pulp? And all those sojers blasted to nothing? What about all those that there's nothing left of to burn or bury? (p. 36).

The voice taunts the boy with the folly of his belief in redemption, mocks his searching for a sign from God, and sneers at his "hunger in the gut" as a case of worms

—an ironic image in that it is traditionally associated with mortality and with Satan.

The most important effect of the voice is to cause Tarwater to doubt the imperatives given to him by his great-uncle, particularly in regard to the baptism of Bishop. "Had it not been for the sustaining voice of the stranger who accompanies him," says Sister M. Simon Nolde, "Tarwater would have succumbed to one of the many temptations to baptize Bishop."[29] She explains that one of the opportunities, in a park near a fountain of running water, is accompanied by the searched-for sign for which he had asked: "Tarwater felt, as they had entered the park, a 'hush in his blood and a stillness in the atmosphere as if the air were being purged for the approach of revelation.' "[30] As Bishop is illuminated by a sudden shaft of light breaking from the clouds, the voice is significantly absent: "His friend was silent as if in the felt presence, he dared not raise his voice" (p. 164). Rayber snatches the child from the water before Tarwater can act; after this failure Tarwater speaks to his image in the water to say that he would drown the child rather than baptize him, and the image speaking in the voice of the stranger-friend answers him: "Drown him then" (p. 165). Sister Nolde points out that "The idea of drowning Bishop is renewed by the stranger when, on arrival at the lodge, he insistently says to Tarwater: 'Don't you have to do something at last, one thing to prove you ain't going to do another?' "[31] Although Tarwater does baptize Bishop in the lake be-

29. *"The Violent Bear It Away: A Study in Imagery," Xavier University Studies*, I (Spring 1962), 187.
30. *Ibid.*
31. *Ibid.*, p. 188.

hind the Cherokee Lodge, he drowns him as well. Thinking back on this event, Tarwater remembers that the voice of his friend has counseled him, "Be a man. It's only one dimwit you have to drown" (p. 215). At this time the devil has become visible as well as audible to Tarwater, and his appearance is malign and voracious:

> The boy looked up into his friend's eyes, bent upon him, and was startled to see that in the peculiar darkness, they were violet-colored, very close and intense, and fixed on him with a peculiar look of hunger and attraction. He turned his head away, unsettled by their attention (pp. 214–215).

The recollection of these details of his failure is horrifying to Tarwater, and he decisively exorcises his devil: "Suddenly in a high raw voice the defeated boy cried out the words of baptism, shuddered, and opened his eyes. He heard the sibilant oaths of his friend fading away on the darkness" (p. 216). Even though he is temporarily "defeated," Tarwater remains torn between his attraction to the Holy and his attraction to and dependence upon the voice of the devil. At one point he calls upon the devil when an old woman near Powderhead scorns him for having deserted his dead great-uncle's body: "he seeks the help of his internal counselor to provide him with words, but to his horror an obscenity rushes from his lips. Shocked, he saw the moment lost" (p. 225).

His final encounter with the devil is highly significant in that it bears out the prophetic warning about such things given to him by Mason Tarwater and, too, in that it enables Tarwater to recognize the thoroughly evil nature of his friend and mentor. In this instance, the devil appears in the flesh as the driver of a "lavender and cream-colored car" who stops his car to give Tarwater a ride. Although he feels that the man is vaguely familiar, Tarwater does not recognize him for what he is; he accepts the man's cigarettes and his whiskey, which Tarwater observes is thicker than any he had known before. When Tarwater loses consciousness because of the drugged whiskey, he is taken into the woods and violated. Like the devouring satanic figure in "Good Country People," this homosexual carries away tokens of his conquest—Tarwater's hat and the corkscrew bottle-opener given to him by Rayber. As the man leaves "His delicate skin had acquired a faint pink tint as if he had refreshed himself on blood" (p. 231).

Ironically, the objects carried away symbolize not Tarwater's soul but his former self in its inability to say no to the devil and yes to the demands of God as taught to him by his great-uncle. When Tarwater awakens, he clothes the nakedness of his new self only haphazardly and violently purges the area of the evil presence by setting fire to every place his enemy might have touched. Later he comes to Powderhead, and the voice insidiously begins once again. Tarwater, however, recognizes the pervasive odor of the man in the lavander shirt. Without hesitation he fiercely shakes himself free and sets fire to the spot between him and the voice, creating "a rising wall of fire between him and the grinning presence" (p. 238). Only after this final exorcism is the boy enabled to proceed with his mission, to set his face "toward the dark city, where the children of God lay sleeping" (p. 243).

Surely one would not be so mistaken as to take these

devils in Flannery O'Connor's fiction as "this or that psychological tendency." She identifies them quite clearly as denizens of hell bent upon leading one into error and devouring his soul. They represent the utmost in the spiritual corruption which she knows must be made convincing if grace is to have meaning.

Chapter **3** The
Presence
of
Grace

THE proliferation of
the lost and the damned in Flannery O'Connor's stories
and novels should not create the impression that she is
preoccupied with evil, for she has often repeated her
belief that life "has, for all its horror, been found by
God to be worth dying for."[1] In "The Fiction Writer
and His Country" she explains her understanding of
the relationship between these horrors and the affirma-
tive aspects of her themes:

St. Cyril of Jerusalem, in instructing catechumens, wrote:
"The dragon sits by the side of the road, watching those
who pass. Beware lest he devour you. We go to the Father of
Souls, but it is necessary to pass by the dragon." No matter
what form the dragon may take, it is of this mysterious passage past him, or into his jaws, that stories of any depth will
always be concerned to tell, and this being the case, it requires considerable courage at any time, in any country, not
to turn away from the storyteller.[2]

1. Flannery O'Connor, "The Church and the Fiction Writer,"
America, March 30, 1957, p. 733.
2. Flannery O'Connor, "The Fiction Writer and His Country," *The Living Novel: A Symposium,* edited by Granville Hicks,
p. 164.

Although she was wary of didactic or merely "edifying" fiction,[3] nearly all the drama of her stories takes place along this road to salvation. The central mystery of this drama is a man's ability to save his soul by accepting the gift of God's love for him as expressed through Christ's death on the cross. The offer of this love or charity is perpetually renewed in the sacraments and in nature— the world at large and man's individual experience of it. Acceptance of this divine love, either consciously or unknowingly through the will, is spoken of as grace, the term then including God's love for man and man's coming to love God. God's gift is at once love itself and His bestowal upon man of the faculty of love, enabling man to recognize God's love when it is offered. Grace is, therefore, supernatural; it is above man's natural sphere of life, and he may, in his natural sphere, accept or reject the offer.[4]

Although the effect of grace in men's lives is apparent in certain of Flannery O'Connor's characters, she is far more interested in the junctures in men's lives when grace is made available to them and the drama of their decision regarding the offer. In a letter to Andrew Lytle, dated February 4, 1960, Miss O'Connor says:

I have got to the point now where I keep thinking more and more about the presentation of love and charity, or better call it grace, as love suggests tenderness, whereas grace can be violent or would have to be to compete with the kind of evil I can make concrete. . . .

3. Sister Mary Alice, O. P., "My Mentor, Flannery O'Connor," *Saturday Review,* May 29, 1965, p. 25.
4. N. G. M. Van Doornik, S. Jelsma, A. Van De Lisdonk, *A Handbook of the Catholic Faith,* pp. 202–204.

There is a moment of grace in most of the stories or a moment where it is offered, and is usually rejected.[5]

Flannery O'Connor did not take lightly the pervasiveness of this subject in her fiction; she was quite aware that such a theme was fraught with problems, as "The Church and the Fiction Writer" attests: "Part of the complexity of the problem for the Catholic fiction-writer will be the presence of grace as it appears in nature, and what matters for him here is that his faith not become detached from his dramatic sense and from his vision of what is."[6] She felt that the story must succeed in itself apart from its theological implications; the extra dimension arising from the Christian writer's orthodoxy must, therefore, be apparent in a sound dramatic presentation, not applied to the story for the sake of edification, and not achieved through gratuitous and tortured indirection. Contributing to a discussion of the eucharistic symbol, she once remarked, "If it were only a symbol, I'd say to hell with it."[7] Of course she used

5. Letter from Flannery O'Connor to Andrew Lytle, February 4, 1960, Tennessee State Library and Archives, Nashville, Tennessee.

That the offered grace "is usually rejected" may be explained in two ways: (1) She is referring, I believe, to the numerous minor characters as well as the major ones who reject God's grace—those discussed in the previous chapter. (2) In the earlier collection of short stories, major characters who reject grace slightly outnumber those who accept it, whereas in the later stories, those collected in *Everything That Rises Must Converge* (as the very title suggests) show a remarkable preponderance of major characters who recognize grace and accept it, as do the major characters in both novels.

6. P. 734.

7. Quoted by Robert Fitzgerald, "Introduction," *Everything That Rises Must Converge,* by Flannery O'Connor, p. xiii.

such symbolism frequently, but not in such a way as to obscure meaning and, most important, not without meaning the metaphor; the opportunities for grace and the epiphanies in her stories are usually plain, direct, and clearly identifiable. They are firmly founded in the action of the narrative. "If nothing happened," she once said, "there's no story."[8] Her theory is borne out in stories which succeed admirably on a secular level but which yield greater riches for the reader who is receptive to the presence of grace.

Just as all of the characters in Flannery O'Connor's works are not clearly conceived of in terms of religious meaning, all of those who relate to it are not depicted at the moment of religious choice. Some are among the lost because their invincible ignorance precludes the understanding that man is capable of a spiritual or supernatural condition—Rayber's father, Mrs. Leora Watts, and Harry Ashfield's parents. Their counterparts among those who live in grace are characters reckoned baptismally innocent by virtue of their failure to arrive at a condition in which reason allows them to make choices. The church places infants up to seven years of age and insane adults in this category. Mrs. Turpin's vision in "Revelation" revealed to her such figures among the "vast horde of souls . . . rumbling toward heaven"—"battalions of freaks and lunatics shouting and clapping and leaping like frogs."[9]

8. *Ibid.,* p. xv.
9. Flannery O'Connor, *Everything That Rises Must Converge,* p. 217. Further quotations from this work will be identified with the abbreviation *Everything* and a page number in parentheses.

Lucynell Crater in "The Life You Save May Be Your Own" is an excellent example of the baptismally innocent. A deaf mute with poor eyesight, she cannot see Mr. Shiftlet, a vagrant looking for work, as he approaches the porch where she and her mother are sitting. She is "a large girl in a short blue organdy dress," who, sensing the man, "jumped up and began to stamp and point and make excited speechless sounds."[10] Lucynell's simple-mindedness is overshadowed, however, by the significance of her innocence. Although she is thirty years old, her mother tells Mr. Shiftlet that she is fifteen or sixteen, knowing that "because of her innocence it was impossible to guess" (*Good Man,* p. 61). Her mother values her as a "casket of jewels," an image which associates her with the kingdom of heaven described in the New Testament: "Again, the kingdom of heaven is like unto a merchant man, seeking goodly pearls: Who, when he had found one pearl of great price, went and sold all that he had, and bought it" (Matt. 13:45–46). In Revelation 21:9–21 the coming Holy City is described largely in terms of precious stones. Further, the events of "The Life You Save May Be Your Own" bear out the Biblical injunction, "Give not that which is holy unto the dogs, neither cast ye your pearls before swine, lest they trample them under their feet, and turn again and rend you" (Matt. 7:6). Lucynell's mother, "ravenous for a son-in-law," barters away her daughter to Mr. Shiftlet; he takes the old woman's car, which he has repaired, and her money for

10. Flannery O'Connor, *A Good Man Is Hard to Find,* p. 53. Further quotations from this work will be identified with the abbreviation *Good Man* and a page number in parentheses.

a honeymoon, but he then abandons Lucynell in a roadside restaurant called the Hot Spot.

As the waiter looks at the sleeping girl's pink-gold hair and half-shut eyes, as "blue as a peacock's neck," he observes that "She looks like an angel of Gawd" (p. 66). Not only does she embody grace through her innocence, she is also Mr. Shiftlet's opportunity to accept grace—an opportunity which he rejects. His complete awareness of his action is indicated by his transference of the waiter's phrase from Lucynell to his mother, all the while thinking of his abandonment of the girl: "My mother was a angel of Gawd. . . . He took her from heaven and giver to me and I left her" (p. 67). As the title of the story indicates, it is not Lucynell's life that he must save, but his own.

An association between madness and religion is not unusual in Flannery O'Connor's works. Although the only truly feeble-minded character in *The Violent Bear It Away* is the child Bishop Rayber, others who are strongly religious are often taken to be lunatics or morons. Mason Tarwater's nephew, Rayber, at fourteen screams at his uncle: "You're crazy, you're crazy, you're a liar, you have a head full of crap, you belong in a nut house!"[11] Rayber's mother, Mason Tarwater's own sister, had had the old man committed to an insane asylum when he made it a custom to "shout and prophesy" before her house, exhorting her to turn from her life of sin and accept Jesus. He compares his four years there to Ezekiel's forty days in the pit and finally comes

11. Flannery O'Connor, *The Violent Bear It Away*, p. 186. Further quotations from this work will be identified with the abbreviation *Violent* and a page number in parentheses.

to realize "that the way for him to get out was to stop
prophesying on the ward" (*Violent,* p. 62). Later, Rayber threatens his uncle for much the same reasons, "I'll
have you put back in the asylum where you belong" (p.
33). Rayber rationalizes his early belief in the old man
as an attraction "to mad eyes. A grown person could
have resisted. A child couldn't. Children are cursed with
believing" (pp. 170–171). At times when Rayber des-
pairs of rehabilitating young Tarwater, he refers to the
boy in similar fashion, calling him at one point a "goddam backwoods imbecile" (p. 147).

Although to others Tarwater and his uncle appear
insane because they are genuinely God-driven, Bishop,
who is actually imbecilic, is brought to the state of grace
through baptism; from the beginning he is regarded as
one surrounded by an aura of religious mystery. His
generally diaphanous appearance is much like Lucynell
Crater's: like hers his hair is "pink," his complexion
very light; his eyes are grey like old Tarwater's and
seem to go "down and down into two pools of light" (p.
23). This image of divine light is repeated in plainer
fashion on one of the occasions when Tarwater intends
to baptize Bishop as he stands in the pool of a park
fountain: "Then the light, falling more gently, rested
like a hand on the child's white head. His face might
have been a mirror where the sun had stopped to watch
its reflection" (p. 164). When Rayber, Tarwater, and
Bishop are checking in at the Cherokee Lodge, the
woman at the desk reprimands Tarwater for mistreat-
ing the child, her words indicating the traditional reverence in which such people are held: " 'mind how you
talk to one of them there, you boy. . . . That there

kind,' she said, looking at him fiercely as if he had
profaned the holy" (p. 155).

Perhaps the most startling and convincing evidence
of Bishop's essential innocence even before his baptism
is to be found in his quasi-resurrection. As Rayber attempts euthanasia by drowning his own child, Bishop
resists fiercely: "The face under the water was wrath-
fully contorted, twisted by some primeval rage to save
itself" (p. 142). Although Rayber persists and succeeds,
in a moment of agony he drags the drowned boy to
shore, where he is brought back to life through artificial
respiration. This incongruous sequence of death followed by rebirth into natural life is inversely repeated
when Tarwater later baptizes Bishop into spiritual life
eternal and subsequently ends his natural life by
drowning him. Thus the grace attendant upon Bishop's
condition throughout the novel is made virtual by the
baptismal innocence achieved at the moment of his
death.

Because his "normal way of looking on Bishop was as
an x signifying the general hideousness of fate" (p. 113),
Rayber adamantly resists the notion that God places
value upon the life of an idiot; instead of admitting
that the maimed are so because of man's original sin, he
perversely believes that God created Bishop in His own
image. Mason Tarwater is closer to the truth in his
observation that Bishop's condition attests to God's om-
niscience in giving Rayber a child whom he could not
corrupt, although there is as much pure rhetoric as
theology in his remark. However, only urgency and
religious concern mark the old man's wish to baptize
Bishop; he looks upon him as "an unspeakable mys-

tery" (p. 32), not as an indication of the hideousness of fate: "Precious in the sight of the Lord even an idiot" (p. 33). These two characters are often linked by frequent references to their uncanny resemblance to each other: "Bishop looked like the old man grown backwards to the lowest form of innocence" (p. 111). Both of them are described as having fish-colored eyes, the attribute carrying its traditional Christian association with the miracle of Christ's feeding of the multitude, a recurrent image throughout the novel.

Although the younger Tarwater is frequently contemptuous of Bishop almost to the point of revulsion, his attitude toward him is generally that of his great-uncle, whose injunctions to baptize the idiot he carries out in spite of himself. Even his first encounter with Bishop over the telephone, however, disconcerts Tarwater by its significance to him; when Bishop answers the telephone and only breathes into it with "a kind of bubbling noise," Tarwater holds the receiver to his ear and stands "blankly as if he had received a revelation he could not yet decipher. He seemed to have been stunned by some deep internal blow that had not yet made its way to the surface of his mind" (p. 83). At the first meeting of the two, Bishop, "dim and ancient, like a child who had been a child for centuries," is living, undeniable proof that Tarwater must obey his uncle and that he must follow Christ:

Tarwater clenched his fists. He stood like one condemned, waiting at the spot of execution. Then the revelation came, silent, implacable, direct as a bullet. He did not look into the eyes of any fiery beast or see a burning bush. He only knew, with a certainty sunk in despair, that he was expected

to baptize the child he saw and begin the life his great-uncle
had prepared him for. He knew that he was called to be a
prophet and that the ways of his prophecy would not be remarkable. His black pupils, glassy and still, reflected depth
on depth his own stricken image of himself, trudging into
the distance in the bleeding stinking mad shadow of Jesus,
until at last he received his reward, a broken fish, a multiplied loaf (p. 91).

Just as Bishop is linked with Mason Tarwater in Christian terms, their oneness in charity and grace is joined
by Tarwater as a firm bond grows between him and
Bishop. Tarwater's humility before Bishop and his love
for him are indicated on one occasion when Tarwater
kneels down to tie the boy's shoelaces. Later, Rayber
notices with envy that Tarwater gently places his hand
on Bishop's neck as he leads him out, and that, paradoxically reversing their roles, Bishop seems to be leading,
to have made a capture. Rayber watches them as they
stand side by side: "—the two figures, hatted and some-
how ancient, bound together by some necessity of nerve
that excluded him" (p. 196).

Bishop's own actions also reveal his residence in grace
or the presence of God's prevenient grace within him,
moving his will unfreely, inclining it to God.[12] When he
sees Tarwater for the first time, Tarwater knows "that
the child *recognized* him" (pp. 92–93). (This rare instance of Flannery O'Connor's use of italics indicates
the importance she attaches to this detail.) Bishop
reaches out to touch Tarwater on many occasions, re-
minding one of the many instances in which the lame,

12. This definition of prevenient grace is taken from: Donald
Attwater (editor), *A Catholic Dictionary*, p. 217.

the sick, and the possessed sought contact with Christ in hopes of being miraculously healed. There is some relevance, too, in Sumner Ferris's remark upon the significance of the names of the two boys: "One far-fetched but attractive observation may be made about these two names, that although Bishop Berkeley was a famous empirical philosopher, he nevertheless attributed almost magic powers to tarwater."[13] Further, Bishop is delighted with water and strongly attracted to it: "as soon as the dim-witted boy saw the water, he gave a whoop and galloped off toward it, flapping his arms like something released from a cage " (*Violent*, p. 164) . Finally water administered by Tarwater releases Bishop in a twofold manner from the cage of his mortality.

The old Negro, Astor, in "The Displaced Person," is baptismally innocent neither by age nor mentality, but as a primitive he is in harmony with God's charity as surely as Bishop and Lucynell are. Significantly, Astor is the one character who is absent from the death scene at the conclusion of the story. Thus, he is not linked with the guilt of Mr. Guizac's death. Although it is from this old man that Mrs. McIntyre ultimately learns about Mr. Guizac's plan to marry his cousin to Sulk, Astor declares to her also, somewhat mysteriously, that Mr. Guizac is a special kind of person on the farm and not like the Ringfields, the Collinses, the Garrits, and the Shortleys. Pressed by Mrs. McIntyre, Astor manages to answer without revealing what he knows about Mr. Guizac's plan. The exchange between him and Mrs.

13. "The Outside and the Inside: Flannery O'Connor's *The Violent Bear It Away*," *Critique*, III (Winter-Spring 1960) , p. 19, n. 2.

McIntyre has symbolic overtones relevant to Mr. Guizac's function as a Christlike figure:

"If you know anything he's done that he shouldn't, I expect you to report it to me," she said.
"It warn't like it was what he should ought or oughtn't," he muttered. "It was like what nobody else don't do" (*Good Man*, p. 226).

In creating Astor as a point of reference for Christian virtue, Flannery O'Connor makes him an ancient, almost timeless old man, nearly blind. Having lived on the farm long before Mrs. McIntyre's arrival, Astor passes his wisdom on to her by sitting beneath her window conversing with himself loudly enough for her to hear. He has a primitive apocalyptic view that foresees the coming of the day when the Christian's contempt for worldly goods will become a universal condition equalizing men and bringing order out of chaos: "Judge say he long for the day when he be too poor to pay a nigger to work. . . . Say when that day come, the world be back on its feet" (pp. 224–225). Astor's humility is often evident; he expresses it clearly when reprimanding Sulk for his anger at Mrs. Shortley's hint that Sulk might lose his job because of Mr. Guizac's efficiency: " 'Never mind,' the old man said, 'your place too low for anybody to dispute with you for it' " (p. 213).

Two instances of symbolism bear out Astor's significance in the religious theme of the story. When he is raking with Mrs. McIntyre in the calf barn, "Bars of sunlight fell from the cracked ceiling across his back and cut him in three distinct parts" (p. 224). The second instance of symbolism is even more convincing, for it identifies Astor with the most persistent Christian symbol of the story, the peacock:

Or occasionally he spoke with the peacock. The cock would follow him around the place, his steady eye on the ear of corn that stuck up from the old man's back pocket or he would sit near him and pick himself. Once from the open kitchen door, she [Mrs. McIntyre] had heard him say to the bird, "I remember when it was twenty of you walking about this place and now it's only you and two hens. Crooms it was twelve. McIntyre it was five. You and two hens, now."
And that time she had stepped out of the door onto the porch and said, "MISTER Crooms and MISTER McIntyre! And I don't want to hear you call either of them anything else again. And you can understand this: when that peachicken dies there won't be any replacements" (pp. 227–228).

The irony of this passage is that Astor's permanence and patience are not vulnerable to the hysteria and selfishness of Mrs. McIntyre; for Astor, the loss of the peacocks is merely regrettable, but for Mrs. McIntyre the loss is ultimate. Lucynell and Bishop are defeated temporally, as is Astor, but all of them are superior to defeat by merit of their passive residence in grace.

Astor is not the only character in "The Displaced Person" who resides in grace; Mr. Guizac's religious position in the story, however, is defined more overtly. He is a devout Catholic, fairly uncommon in Flannery O'Connor's work. With the exception of two priests, other specifically religious characters are protestant. Certain characters who profess to be religious are not, but the ones who are sincere are identifiable and obviously presented sympathetically.

Robert Fitzgerald comments, quite accurately, that "The Displaced Person" is not Mr. Guizac's story. He says, "The Pole scarcely appears, his innocence or lack of it is neither here nor there."[14] Although it is not the Pole's story, his innocence is significant, for as Sister M. Joselyn has pointed out in a perceptive article enlarging upon Mr. Fitzgerald's, Mr. Guizac is an "obvious thematic center of the story." She observes that the major characters in the story "range themselves around Mr. Guizac on a descending scale from love to hate,"[15] and that their feelings toward him coincide with their attitude toward the peacock in its traditional symbolization of Christ. She studies in detail "Miss O'Connor's deliberate identification of the Displaced Person and Christ, sometimes directly by means of the prior identification of the peacock with Christ."[16] Mrs. McIntyre, for example, who has little use for the peacocks, says that "Christ was just another D.P.," and in more than one instance the Catholic priest talks of the coming of Christ while Mrs. McIntyre's answers are in terms of the coming of Mr. Guizac, whom at one point she ironically considers to be her pragmatic savior on the farm.[17] The recurrent ironic reactions of Mrs. McIntyre to the displaced person are highly significant indicators of his role as an objectification of the presence of grace; when he arrives, she greets him, not as she would welcome an ordinary

14. "The Countryside and the True Country," *Sewanee Review,* LXX (Summer 1962), 389.
15. "Thematic Centers in 'The Displaced Person,'" *Studies in Short Fiction,* I (Winter 1964), 86.
16. *Ibid.,* p. 90.
17. *Ibid.,* pp. 90–91.

hired hand, but effusively, wearing her best clothes. Before she becomes disenchanted with him, she refers to him as her salvation and as "a kind of miracle" (*Good Man,* p. 230).

Further, Mr. Guizac's own actions indicate his charity: he is devoted to his responsibilities on the farm, he receives frequent visits from the priest, he treats the Negroes with the same dignity and respect accorded to every other person, he is disturbed by the complacency in regard to Sulk's dishonesty when the Negro steals a frying-size turkey, and (although this was his damning error in the eyes of those who perpetrated the religion of the countryside) he wishes to save his young cousin from the European camps for displaced persons by marrying her to Sulk. Like Lucynell Crater and Bishop Rayber, then, Mr. Guizac is not only the repository of grace, but an occasion for the acceptance of grace by others—Mr. and Mrs. Shortley, Mrs. McIntyre, and Sulk. All reject the opportunity. Mrs. Shortley dies at the height of her anger toward him, but the other three participate in his death, at which their "eyes come together in one look that froze them in collusion forever" (*Good Man,* p. 250). Mr. Guizac is last seen as a bloody corpse over whom the priest bends, delivering the last rites of the church.

Only two Catholic priests play active roles in Flannery O'Connor's fiction, Father Flynn in "The Displaced Person," and Father Finn in "The Enduring Chill," both old, both Irish, and both unequivocal points of reference for the presence of grace. Father Flynn in "The Displaced Person" is associated with the peacock in every appearance in the story, once referring to the bird as "The Transfiguration" (*Good Man,* p. 239). He shows remarkable patience with Mrs. McIntyre's exasperating dullness and pragmatism, often diverting his attention from her tirades by admiring the beautiful bird.

Father Flynn is concerned for the welfare of her soul as well as for the Guizacs, the displaced people. To the priest, she is spiritually displaced. Mrs. McIntyre, however, is contemptuous of his attempts to convert her: "After he had got her the Pole, he had used the business introduction to try to convert her—just as she had supposed he would" (pp. 237–238). Like Mrs. Shortley, she considers the Catholic Church to be unreformed, and religion in general to be for social purposes only or for those without brains enough to avoid evil without it. What she takes as a threatening attempt to convert her is to the priest a charitable endeavor—an accepted Christian duty of his role as priest:

She had not asked to be instructed but he instructed anyway, forcing a little definition of one of the sacraments or of some dogma into each conversation he had, no matter with whom. He sat on her porch, taking no notice of her partly mocking, partly outraged expression (pp. 242–243).

Although he takes every opportunity to instruct Mrs. McIntyre in the means of grace, Father Flynn's own grace does not engender itself in her. And yet even after she has betrayed his hope in her charity by allowing the death of Mr. Guizac, the priest's unshakable charity persists as he continues to visit her when she is left alone and bedridden with a nervous affliction.

Father Finn ("from Purrgatory," he introduces himself) in "The Enduring Chill," is, like Father Flynn, old and conventional, concerned with the basic truths of his faith and dismayed at those who live outside the state of grace; he is not a modern liberal Jesuit of the type Asbury Fox had known in the Bohemian circles in New York. In fact, the priest's role is quite clear and the issues in this story are obvious. Asbury Fox is a pitifully immature literary poseur, fearful of his own disillusionment and eager to find solace from someone whom he considers his equal. Mistakenly believing himself to be dying, he chooses to summon a Catholic priest, expecting someone like the Jesuit who acknowledged him in New York at a Zen Buddhist lecture on Vedanta.

Contrary to Asbury's expectations, Father Finn, blind in one eye and somewhat deaf, knows nothing of James Joyce and has little patience with Asbury's pseudo-intellectual, agnostic dialectic. He reprimands the boy for not praying, telling him that "You cannot love Jesus unless you speak to Him" (p. 105). As the priest's indignation at Asbury's impertinence builds until his words are spoken in "a battering voice," he leads the young man through parts of the catechism and warns him of the dangers of ignoring God's grace.

These two Catholic priests are moral and theological referents that cannot be denied or ignored; however, it is more customary in Flannery O'Connor's work to find this function, when it exists, in a Bible Belt Protestant figure, often a self-styled evangelist preacher such as The Reverend Bevel Summers in "The River," and, in Wise Blood, Hazel Motes's grandfather, "a circuit preacher, a waspish old man who had ridden over three counties with Jesus in his head like a stinger."[18] The old man preached from the nose of a Ford automobile, as Haze was later to preach the Church Without Christ from the nose of his Essex; the grandfather's message was, however, strict, fundamental orthodoxy regarding Christ's mission. It is his grandfather's violent words of faith and belief that Haze is fleeing in the novel; the words of salvation and of the acid of God's grace as delivered by the old man burn themselves into Haze's character and constitute an unvoiced, implicit, imperative doctrine which the boy attempts to escape but cannot. With such religious fervor and truth in his background, Hazel is a Christian in spite of himself.

The Carmodys, the missionary family holding meetings at the tabernacle in *The Violent Bear It Away*, serve much the same function as Haze's grandfather does in *Wise Blood* and the Catholic priests in "The Displaced Person" and "The Enduring Chill." Lucette Carmody, the child, is the principal figure; her coarse introduction is given by the evangelist who thinks Jesus "hadda hunch" that little children might lead others to Him. The preacher's platitude that Christ "teaches us wisdom out of the mouths of babes" (*Violent*, p. 124) is borne out, however, and the child herself proclaims more than once, quite justifiably, that "The Holy Word is in my mouth!" (p. 133). She uses one of the novel's central images of the violence of the coming of the kingdom of God—when she claims, "The Word of God is a burning Word to burn you clean . . . ! Be saved in

18. Flannery O'Connor, *Wise Blood*, p. 20. Further quotations from this work will be identified with the abbreviation *WB* and a page number in parentheses.

the Lord's fire or perish in your own!" (pp. 134–135).
The topic of her sermon is love, the love and charity of
God which Flannery O'Connor chooses to call grace.[19]
Lucette's eloquent sermon comes at the center of the
novel, and, along with Mason Tarwater's fervidly religious harangues, it represents the most significant vocal
expression of the Christian values that inform the entire novel.

The other character in *The Violent Bear It Away*
who overtly expresses the overwhelming and violent
nature of God's grace is Mason Tarwater, F. M. Tarwater's great-uncle. The old man considers himself a
prophet; he compares himself to various Old Testament
figures, particularly to Ezekiel and to Elijah, especially
in his function in preparing the way for Elisha, to
whom he compares his great-nephew. He considers the
salvation of the souls of those in his family his responsibility and in carrying out this duty he kidnaps George
Rayber (whom he ultimately fails to win) and Francis
Marion Tarwater (whom he does win, keeping him out
of school and teaching him the history of the world in
his own parochially Christian fashion).

Old Tarwater's role as prophet is not shabby, idle,
and shallow, but truly apocalyptic. As a young man he
had gone to the city to warn the people of the doom
awaiting those who reject Christ as their savior, prophesying the bursting of the sun in the imminent final
holocaust. The failure of his prophecy is attended by
the revelation of his own soul burned clean of its pride
by God's fire:

19. Letter from Flannery O'Connor to Andrew Lytle, *loc. cit.*

[The Sun] rose and set and he despaired of the Lord's listening. Then one morning he saw to his joy a finger of fire coming out of it and before he could turn, before he could shout, the finger had touched him and the destruction he had been waiting for had fallen in his own brain and his own body. His own blood had been burned dry and not the blood of the world.

Having learned much by his own mistakes, he was in a position to instruct Tarwater—when the boy chose to listen —in the hard facts of serving the Lord. . . .

That was not the last time the Lord had corrected the old man with fire, but it had not happened since he had taken Tarwater from the schoolteacher (pp. 5–6).

Mason Tarwater's rhetoric is whirling and angry, but his message is essentially that of Lucette Carmody except for its uniquely masculine tone:

"Ignore the Lord Jesus as long as you can! Spit out the bread of life and sicken on honey. Whom work beckons, to work. Whom blood to blood! Whom lust to lust! Make haste, make haste. Fly faster and faster. Spin yourselves in a frenzy, the time is short! The Lord is preparing a prophet. The Lord is preparing a prophet with fire in his hand and eye and the prophet is moving toward the city with his warning. The prophet is coming with the Lord's message. 'Go warn the children of God,' saith the Lord, 'of the terrible speed of Justice.' Who will be left? Who will be left when the Lord's mercy strikes?" (p. 60).

Although Mason dies at the beginning of the novel, the essence of these words is repeated constantly through young Tarwater's preoccupation with his great-uncle's charge to him to carry on his mission. The old man is incensed when Rayber ridicules him as a self-appointed prophet, and the validity of old Mason Tarwater's role is established at the end of the novel when his nephew finally surrenders himself to the duties that the old man had expected of him and prepared him for. The boy sees that his hunger "was the same as the old man's and that nothing on earth would fill him. His hunger was so great that he would have eaten all the loaves and fishes after they were multiplied" (p. 241). The triumph is as much Mason's as it is the boy's. The old man is the most extensively developed character who is consistently and unmistakably Christian. It is a grave error to allow the broad good nature of his portrait to minimize the seriousness of his role. Flannery O'Connor has said of him: "Old Tarwater is the hero of 'The Violent Bear It Away,' and I'm right behind him 100 percent."[20]

Such positive figures do not appear in all or even in a majority of Miss O'Connor's fiction; but when they are included, regardless of their quaintness, one must realize her complete sympathy with them.

20. Quoted by Granville Hicks, "A Writer at Home with Her Heritage," *Saturday Review*, May 12, 1962, as reprinted in *The Added Dimension*, p. 258.

Chapter 4   Manifestations of God's Grace

As several critics have noticed, most of Flannery O'Connor's stories follow a pattern, the similarity of which arises largely from her invariably Christian perspective upon the characters and action. The pattern is that of the prototypical Christian experience, moving from the condition of sinfulness to a recognition of sin, repentance for it, confession, penance, and absolution. But as Rainulf Stelzmann has observed, only in the novels is there even a semblance of all stages of this Christian experience.[1] Most of the short stories are constructed in such a way as to dramatize the sinfulness and the need for grace, followed by, near the end of the story, an epiphany in which the main character recognizes his need for re-

1. "Shock and Orthodoxy: An Interpretation of Flannery O'Connor's Novels and Short Stories," *Xavier University Studies,* II (March 1963), 8.

pentance and either accepts or ignores the opportunity. In a few stories there is no indication as to the response of the character to his new insight.

The characters examined previously may be taken as examples of habitual grace—they are static figures, observers, and inspirers who serve largely as foils for the major figures. Those to be considered here, however, are participating, engaged characters whose experiences show the working of prevenient grace—which moves the will spontaneously, making it incline to God—and illuminating grace, by which God enlightens men to bring them nearer to eternal life.

Some O'Connor characters arrive at their epiphanies from a condition of relative innocence or ignorance, without being guilty of active evil or long-standing spiritual pride. Consequently, their illumination is more a coming to knowledge of God's grace than an "entry into the world of guilt and suffering,"[2] a phrase Flannery O'Connor used to denote Julian's final awareness in "Everything That Rises Must Converge." Harry Ashfield in "The River," the twelve-year-old child in "A Temple of the Holy Ghost," Mr. Head and Nelson in "The Artificial Nigger," and Mrs. Flood in *Wise Blood* exemplify this movement from innocence or ignorance to knowledge.

2. Flannery O'Connor, *Everything That Rises Must Converge,* p. 23. Further quotations from this work will be identified with the abbreviation *Everything* and a page number in parentheses.

Harry Ashfield lives in complete ignorance of Christianity, having been reared by heathenish parents who use religious terms only profanely. Harry is pleased to learn from his baby-sitter, Mrs. Connin, "That he had been made by a carpenter named Jesus Christ,"[3] and he is so delighted with *The Life of Jesus Christ for Readers Under Twelve* that he steals the book from Mrs. Connin. The narrowness of the child's past is apparent in his ignorance of the nonurban world to which the baby-sitter takes him; his knowledge of the country is so inadequate that he is unable to avoid being tricked by the Connin children and trampled by a pig. As the name Ashfield connotes, his parents live in an urban spiritual wasteland of cocktail parties, stale cigarette butts on Sunday morning, and windows stained so gray that the sunlight is pale. On the other hand, the sun in the country, a detail that recurs frequently in the story, is brilliant, and in the river where The Reverend Bevel Summers (whose very name carries out the imagery) baptizes the child, "the reflection of the sun was set like a diamond" (*Good Man,* p. 39). The obvious religious significance of this symbolism is Harry's journey from the darkness of ignorance into the light of God's grace. This imagery of light parallels the child's changing his name to Bevel, thus renouncing his identity with the Ashfields.

Another significant pattern of imagery in "The River," and one which has importance throughout

3. Flannery O'Connor, *A Good Man Is Hard to Find,* p. 38. Further quotations from this work will be identified with the abbreviation *Good Man* and a page number in parentheses.

Flannery O'Connor's fiction, especially in *The Violent Bear It Away*,[4] relates to food. Its religious meaning in this story is associated both with Harry's need for participation in the Eucharist and, after his baptism, with Harry's spiritual satisfaction—he no longer lives by bread alone. The first of these meanings appears when Mrs. Connin asks Harry what affliction he has that the healer might remedy: " 'I'm hungry,' he decided finally" (p. 33). The comment on the child's Sunday breakfast (two crackers spread with anchovy paste and ginger ale) clearly indicates the boy's lack of spiritual satisfaction: "There was very little to do at any time but eat; however, he was not a fat boy" (p. 49). The second meaning of food symbolism is found in Mr. Paradise's attempt to save Harry from deliberately drowning himself to find "the Kingdom of Christ in the river" (p. 51). The old man has "a peppermint stick, a foot long and two inches thick," which he futilely waves as an enticement to the child as he dashes to rescue him. Pointing out symbolically the irrelevance of earthly food to Harry, the candy appears to him only as "a red and white club" (p. 52).

The reasoning that leads to Harry Ashfield's self-im-

4. In *The Violent Bear It Away* Tarwater suffers through the novel from insatiable hunger and a paradoxical aversion to food, the significance of which is clearly established by allusions to Christ's feeding of the multitude. Because Tarwater's hunger is for spiritual sustenance, he cannot be satisfied by worldly food. At the conclusion of the novel this imagery is resolved when Tarwater sees a vision of the multitude being fed and is turned by his hunger to the religious role assigned to him by his uncle and implicitly by God.

posed death is twofold. First, he sees the kingdom under the river as a desirable alternative to the wasteland in which he lives. " 'Yes,' the child said, and thought, I won't go back to the apartment then, I'll go under the river" (p. 44). When he leaves the apartment on Sunday morning to return to the river, he does not take a suitcase "because there was nothing from there he wanted to keep" (p. 50). The world created for the child by his parents was not only heathen, it was without love or sincerity. Coming from an environment in which "everything was a joke" (p. 44), Harry is deeply impressed by the seriousness of the faith-healing service and his own baptism.

The second aspect of the reasoning behind Harry's fatal plunge into the river is his own fear that the mere outward sign of baptism, his brief immersion by the Reverend Bevel Summers, is insufficient for the full realization of what he in his literal-mindedness expects from the sacrament. "He intended not to fool with preachers any more but to Baptize himself and to keep on going this time until he found the Kingdom of Christ in the river" (p. 51). When Harry's own urge for self-preservation makes his immersion difficult, he fears that the promises of Mrs. Connin and the preacher in regard to the rewards of baptism may be "just another joke." However, the current finally takes him with a "long gentle hand," and the child's momentary surprise is followed by the assured feeling "that he was getting somewhere, [and] all his fury and his fear left him" (p. 52). Robert McCown sums up the total effect of this story when he says that it "achieves an effect of exquisite sadness, but then of exaltation, as the reader realizes that the forces working in the child's pilgrim soul were none other than divine grace."[5]

Harry Ashfield undergoes the initiatory rite of the church and is thus made, as the preacher says, to count. The twelve-year old girl in "A Temple of the Holy Ghost" undergoes the next stage of a Christian's life in the church, the sacrament of confirmation, signifying the bodily and spiritual maturity of the communicant and his reception of the Holy Spirit. When the child's mother impresses Joanne and Susan, the flighty and shallow girls from the convent school, with the actuality that their bodies are temples of the Holy Ghost—they have been highly amused at the idea—the child is moved to begin understanding the meaning of this theological concept: "I am a Temple of the Holy Ghost, she said to herself, and was pleased with the phrase. It made her feel as if somebody had given her a present" (*Good Man*, p. 88).

The success of the story depends partly upon its accurate rendering of the curious combination of childishness and maturity—especially in a religious context —typical of a twelve-year-old girl. Childishly she is highly amused by the physical conditions of the people around her, even though she herself has "fat cheeks and . . . braces . . . in her mouth [that] glared like tin" (p. 86). She notices that Susan is skinny and Joanne talks through her nose and turns purple in patches when she laughs. Miss Kirby, "a long-faced blonde schoolteacher who boarded with them" (p. 86), is an object of much fun to the child because she is a pathetic old maid who does not understand, or perhaps will not acknowledge, the child's mocking remarks about her only suitor, Mr. Cheatam, another ludicrous human body but also theologically a temple of the Holy Ghost. Alonzo Myers, the taxi driver who drives the family to and from Mount Saint Scholastica to get Joanne and Susan, serves the same thematic function as the girls, Miss Kirby, and Mr. Cheatam. Alonzo is not a freak, but his physical characteristics are sufficiently grotesque to require extraordinary powers of faith to relate him, as one surely must, to the theological point of the story:

> He was an eighteen-year-old boy who weighed two hundred and fifty pounds and worked for the taxi company and he was all you could get to drive you anywhere. He smoked or rather chewed a short black cigar and he had a round sweaty chest that showed through the yellow nylon shirt he wore. When he drove all the windows of the car had to be open (p. 87).

In spite of her immaturity and her caustic sense of humor, the child is keenly aware of the inexplicable mystery of the human condition. When her mother expresses pity for Miss Kirby at having to ride in an automobile "that smells like the last circle in hell" (p. 89), the child thinks of the old maid as a temple of the Holy Ghost. The beginning of the child's most significant insight in this regard is introduced when Joanne and Susan, having been to the county fair with Wendell and Cory Wilkins, reluctantly tell her about the hermaphrodite which displayed itself to an audience separated by a curtain, the men and women on opposite sides. Its speech is the same on both sides of the curtain:

> "God made me thisaway and if you laugh he may strike you the same way. This is the way He wanted me to be and I

ain't disputing His way. I'm showing you because I got to
make the best of it. I expect you to act like ladies and gen-
tlemen. I never done it to myself nor had a thing to do with
it but I'm making the best of it. I don't dispute hit" (p.
97).

Because of the presence of this sideshow, the ministers
of the town protest loudly enough to have the fair
closed. Ironically, the implicit theme of the hermaphrodite's spiel and the meaning of its very grotesqueness is that man, for all his physical corruption, is the
residing place of God in the world. Extensive connec-
tions are drawn between the child's growing understanding of her own religious significance and the hermaphrodite at the fair. She imagines that the men in
the audience were solemn, as if "they were in church,"
that the women watched expectantly as if "waiting for
the first note of the piano to begin the hymn," and
that the hermaphrodite's speech was delivered as a
litany, the audience answering "amen" to the imagina-
tively heightened speech of the freak.

The conclusion of the story makes specific the mysterious identity of man's body with God's being by presenting through the child's mind the convergence of the
body of Christ, as the Host in the Catholic service of
benediction, and the body of the hermaphrodite. At
Mount Saint Scholastica, Joanne and Susan, the child,
and her mother are escorted into benediction by a
moon-faced nun. The child kneels and, after expelling
"ugly thoughts" from her mind, realizes that she is "in
the presence of God."

Her mind began to get quiet and then empty but when the
priest raised the monstrance with the Host shining ivory-
colored in the center of it, she was thinking of the tent at
the fair that had the freak in it. The freak was saying, "I

don't dispute hit. This is the way He wanted me to be" (p. 100).

Although the child is not so changed that on the way home in the taxicab after the service she sees Alonzo Myers as anything but fat and repulsive, her sacramental apprehension of the sunset symbolically verifies her spiritual maturity: "The sun was a huge red ball like an elevated Host drenched in blood and when it sank out of sight, it left a line in the sky like a red clay road hanging over the trees" (p. 101).

The principal theme of "The Artificial Nigger" is also the transition of the main characters from innocence into sacramental knowledge; Mr. Head and his grandson, Nelson, whom he has raised from infancy, lose their mild but rivalrous familial pride and enter into a richer, more respectful relationship with each other. The story almost literally objectifies Christ's paradoxical teaching that one must lose his life to save it; the two rustic main characters take an excursion to Atlanta, become lost, then alienated from each other, and, in finding their common way out of Atlanta, become reconciled, returning to their true backwoods country with humility and new knowledge of themselves.

Mr. Head and Nelson's pride is not spiritual pride, such as that of Milton's Satan or Doctor Faustus, or that of George Rayber, Mrs. McIntyre, or Mrs. Cope. The pride apparent in Mr. Head and Nelson is venial sin, for its gravity is manifest only in the largeness of the charity which it precipitates, not in the extent to which God could be displeased with either of them for it. For example, each wants to awaken before the other, and

each resolutely refuses to admit his fallibility in regard
to the most banal everyday issues. While the old man
considers himself "a suitable guide for the young"
(*Good Man*, p. 102) and thinks that "the boy would at
last find out that he was not as smart as he thought he
was" (p. 104), Nelson is "a child who was never satisfied until he had given an impudent answer" (p. 104).
The similarities of their temperaments suggest their
equal need for humility and insight:

They were grandfather and grandson but they looked
enough alike to be brothers and brothers not too far apart
in age, for Mr. Head had a youthful expression by daylight,
while the boy's look was ancient, as if he knew everything
already and would be pleased to forget it (p. 105).

As the title indicates, the chief imagery of the story
revolves around the Negro. In the mountainous Georgia county where Mr. Head and Nelson live, there are
no Negroes. Mr. Head frequently reminds the boy that
he is completely ignorant of Negroes, although Nelson
contends that he must have seen many of them as an
infant since he was born in Atlanta. When a Negro
man and his family walk past them in the train, Mr.
Head asks Nelson, "What was that?" persisting with
questions so as to leave no doubt about Nelson's ignorance. The accumulation of the child's answers, however, constitutes a foreshadowing of the ultimate and
unanswerable question concerning the mystery of man's
worldly existence. Nelson's replies are: "A man"; "a fat
man"; "an old man" (p. 110). Mr. Head finally proclaims triumphantly, "That was a nigger." The Negro
man has "a heavy sad face" but his general bearing,

though it borders on self-conscious elegance, is dignified
and imposing. When Mr. Head and his grandson see
the Negro family in a segregated section of the dining
car, the old man explains to Nelson proudly, "They
rope them off" (p. 112). The remarkably impersonal
quality in *them* reveals Mr. Head's attitude that Negroes are only things, not human beings.

The two white characters later feel the existentialist
sense of isolation which attends such an analysis of
others, when they become aware of themselves as mere
objects under the gaze of Negroes. As Mr. Head and
Nelson wander directionlessly in the Negro section of
Atlanta, they become self-consciously aware that "Black
eyes in black faces were watching them from every
direction" (p. 117). A foreshadowing of the knowledge
that grows into epiphany is apparent, however, when
Nelson's fortune from a penny-scale, "You have a great
destiny ahead of you but beware of dark women" (p.
115), is fulfilled. Ironically, they should both have been
wary of their own ignorance, not of the dark woman.
The sensual Negress whom Nelson asks for directions
gives them correctly, but Mr. Head and the boy misin-
terpret them.

This woman is additionally significant in that she
becomes a crystallizing agent for Nelson's emergent
identity as a man. As the sense of being lost engulfs him,
the image of the Negress as a protective mother and a
sexually exciting mistress in one suddenly enthralls
him. He admires her physically and wishes her to pick
him up and embrace him. "He felt as if he were reeling
down through a pitchblack tunnel" (p. 119). Mr. Head

scorns his grandson's behavior, telling Nelson that he has no sense; he then shows his own ignorance of the city by following the trolley tracks in the wrong direction.

As they sit down to rest, Nelson falls asleep; Mr. Head hides, awakens the child with a noise, and frantically chases the frightened Nelson, whose desperate flight ends in a collision with an elderly woman carrying groceries. She threatens Nelson with the police; the boy clutches his grandfather only to be denied: " 'This is not my boy,' [Mr. Head] said. 'I never seen him before' " (p. 123).

The separation is especially severe for Nelson: it separates him and his grandfather physically by at least twenty paces; it towers over Mr. Head's almost abject, though roundabout, attempts to assuge the wound with offers of spigot water and Coca-Cola; it even brings about, just before reconciliation, Mr. Head's burying his stiff pride to ask for directions back to the train station. The breach between them is finally not so much forgiven as made insignificant by their common recognition of a symbol leveling them in their misunderstanding and guilt, revealing to them the oneness of men in guilt, ignorance, and the suffering of injustice —an ill-made, battered, tasteless statue of a Negro boy holding a piece of watermelon.

Mr. Head and Nelson are transfixed; the description of them reiterates, in contrast to their recent alienation, the uncanny likeness between them, and, significantly, the same sort of agelessness attributed to the plaster figure. They see the "artificial nigger" as some great mystery, some monument to another's victory that brought them together in their common defeat. They could feel it dissolving their differences like an action of mercy. Mr. Head had never known before what mercy felt like because he had been too good to deserve any, but he felt he knew now. He looked at Nelson and understood that he must say something to the child to show that he was still wise and in the look the boy returned he saw a hungry need for that assurance. Nelson's eyes seemed to implore him to explain once and for all the mystery of existence (p. 128).

The meaning in "The Artificial Nigger" is most clearly explained in the unmistakable words of the story itself:

Mr. Head stood very still and felt the action of mercy touch him again but this time he knew that there were no words in the world that could name it. He understood that it grew out of agony, which is not denied to any man and which is given in strange ways to children. He understood it was all a man could carry into death to give his Maker and he suddenly burned with shame that he had so little of it to take with him. He stood appalled, judging himself with the thoroughness of God, while the action of mercy covered his pride like a flame and consumed it. He had never thought himself a great sinner before but he saw now that his true depravity had been hidden from him lest it cause him despair. He realized that he was forgiven for sins from the beginning of time, when he had conceived in his own heart the sin of Adam, until the present, when he had denied poor Nelson. He saw that no sin was too monstrous for him to claim as his own, and since God loved in proportion as He forgave, he felt ready at that instant to enter Paradise (pp. 128–129).

Although Mr. Head's epiphany in "The Artificial Nigger" is not likely to be misunderstood, it is not surprising that some critics have mistakenly taken Mrs.

Flood, Hazel Motes's landlady in *Wise Blood,* to be a
voracious, avaricious woman steeped in evil,[6] "a carica-
tured portrait of Bible Belt morality."[7] Mrs. Flood,
however, is also in a relatively neutral moral situation;
her evil is the practical concern with herself and her
needs, typifying her insensitivity to the absolute morality of sacrificing one's self for all other men. Her petty
conniving to get more of Haze's government check by
raising his rent is counterbalanced by her frequent display of kindness, sympathy, and generosity toward him.
Thus the characterization reveals culpability but not
irredeemable malice. Mrs. Flood undergoes conversion
progressively as she witnesses Hazel Motes's Oedipus-
like blinding of himself. When he tells her of his intention, she is completely unable to understand the meaning of it. Her own solution to "feeling that bad" would
have been suicide, she thinks, and one sees a parallel to
Jocasta in *Oedipus Rex* (which Flannery O'Connor
read for the first time during the writing of this novel),[8]
who hangs herself rather than live with the terrifying
knowledge of her wretchedness. Unlike Jocasta, Mrs.
Flood is not aware of her wretchedness and so lives to
pursue greater knowledge of herself—and ultimately of
God—being carried inexorably on by the nagging suspicion that Haze, though blind, sees something that she
does not. As in Sophocles' tragedy, sight imagery is
highly significant; Mrs. Flood considers herself to be

6. Jonathan Baumbach, *The Landscape of Nightmare,* p. 96.
7. Melvin J. Friedman, "Flannery O'Connor: Another Legend
in Southern Fiction," *English Journal,* LI (April 1962), 241.
8. Robert Fitzgerald, "Introduction," *Everything That Rises
Must Converge,* p. xvi.

"clear-sighted": "She didn't like the thought that something was being put over her head. She liked the clear
light of day. She liked to see things."[9] Early in this
sequence of the novel, "it occurred to her suddenly that
when she was dead she would be blind too" (*WB*, p.
211), but the meaning of her observation is slow in
coming to her. She begins to study Haze as if he were a
question and imagines that if she were blind she would
listen to the radio, eat cake and ice cream, and soak her
feet; whereas Haze, inexplicably to her, lives an ascetic
life in contempt of the world.

Her movement toward knowledge begins most significantly after Haze explains to her that "If there's no
bottom in your eyes, they hold more," and that she
cannot understand his acts of mortification because,
"You can't see" (p. 222). Although her petulance toward him continues, so does her gradual penetration
into the heart of the mystery that he represents:

She could not make up her mind what would be inside his
head and what out. She thought of her own head as a
switchbox where she controlled from; but with him, she
could only imagine the outside in, the whole black world in
his head and his head bigger than the world, his head big
enough to include the sky and the planets and whatever was
or had been or would be. How would he know if time was
going backwards or forwards or if he was going with it? She
imagined it was like you were walking in a tunnel and all
you could see was a pinpoint of light. She had to imagine
the pinpoint of light; she couldn't think of it at all without
that. She saw it as some kind of star, like the star on Christ-

9. Flannery O'Connor, *Wise Blood*, p. 218. Further quotations
from this work will be identified with the abbreviation *WB* and
a page number in parentheses.

mas cards. She saw him going backwards to Bethlehem and she had to laugh (*WB*, pp. 218–219).

Even though Mrs. Flood is not aware of it, her description of Haze's condition shows almost mystical religious insight in encompassing the divine timelessness and limitlessness of Haze's vision of God.

Her impatience turns to solicitude: she buys two rubber plants to enhance the porch where they sit, tries to interest him in playing the guitar, offers him the money she finds in his trash can, carries tasty dishes to him in his room, and frets over his general welfare. She recognizes, though she expresses it in a "voice of High Sarcasm," that Haze, in spite of the name of his church, demonstrates his belief in Jesus through his unusual behavior. Mrs. Flood's own conversion to Hazel's thinking is foreshadowed by her wish to marry him, not to get his pension or to commit him to the state institution, as she had earlier planned, but to "keep him. Watching his face had become a habit with her; she wanted to penetrate the darkness behind it and see for herself what was there" (p. 225).

Although she broaches her marriage proposition to him as a hedge against the emptiness of the world (" 'If we don't help each other, Mr. Motes, there's nobody to help us, '. . . Nobody. The world is an empty place' " [p. 227]), her ignorance of the place of holiness in matrimony does not diminish her sincerity. Indeed, the imagery suggests the traditional Christian analogy between Christ and the church, Haze in this instance standing as a Christlike bridegroom and Mrs. Flood (her name associating with the descendants of Noah) taking her position as the expectant bride soon to be assimilated into the one flesh of God—the concept that makes marriage a sacrament and extends the bridegroom imagery to approach the significance of the partaking of Christ's body in the Mass. The consummation of the proposed marriage is figuratively accomplished when two policemen bring Hazel's dead body to Mrs. Flood and place it in her bed. "I see you've come home!" she says (p. 231), and talks to him as if he were alive. Only through his death does she understand the meaning of his life, as through Christ's death the universal church finds salvation. As she examines Haze's face, her sight turns inward upon the truth for the first time. Although she stares intently at his eyes, only when she closes her own does she realize the meaning of Hazel's action. Mrs. Flood feels helpless to act upon the truth, but she has witnessed it.

Hazel Motes's conversion is quite different in nature from his landlady's; his change is not one from ignorance or innocence such as hers and that of the others like her. Instead, he is one of a large group of O'Connor characters whose epiphanies follow experiences dominated by entrenched pride, willful sin, deliberate rejection of God, or possibly all three. Francis Marion Tarwater in *The Violent Bear It Away,* Asbury Fox in "The Enduring Chill," Mrs. Turpin in "Revelation," Calhoun and Mary Elizabeth in "The Partridge Festival," Julian in "Everything That Rises Must Converge," and O. E. Parker in "Parker's Back" also experience this kind of epiphany.

At the opening of *Wise Blood,* the very name of

Hazel Motes's evangelical crusade, the Church Without Christ, certifies his vehement disavowal of God's grace. His background includes exposure to stringent religious practice and subsequent traumatic guilt: his stern mother, the evangelist grandfather with Jesus in his head like a stinger, the obscene sideshow at the carnival, Hazel's attempt to purify himself through mortification. Even as a child his ingrained religion has the marks of fear rather than faith; though trying to emulate his grandfather, he feels that he must avoid sin in order to avoid Jesus. Such religious thinking illustrates the profound spiritual pride that leads man to believe himself capable of achieving his own salvation; it is an outstanding heresy in Christian thought. Haze has such "strong confidence in his power to resist evil" (*WB*, p. 157) that Jesus is expelled from his dialectic even before he embraces a dedicated belief in blasphemy and nothingness:

Later he saw Jesus move from tree to tree in the back of his mind, a wild ragged figure motioning him to turn around and come off into the dark where he was not sure of his footing, where he might be walking on the water and not know it and then suddenly know it and drown (*WB*, p. 22).

Even the vestiges of orthodox faith are lost when Haze is in the army. Having carried with him symbols of that faith, "a black Bible and a pair of silver-rimmed spectacles that had belonged to his mother" (p. 23), he is rigidly defensive of his soul against the threats of the government, foreign places to which he might be sent, and priests taking orders from the Pope. But he is not immune to the skepticism of other soldiers who inform him that he has no soul. Wanting to believe them and suffering the physical and psychological wounds of war, Haze gets rid of his soul by converting his proud heterodox belief "to nothing instead of to evil" (p. 24).

When Haze returns home to Eastrod, Tennessee, aware that all those of his family who have created his character and against whom he has rebelled are dead, the next stage in the almost medieval drama of his soul's fortune occurs. His disappointment upon finding only an empty skeleton of a house remaining suggests that he expected to find the dead resurrected, as he had expected both his father and mother to rise up in their coffins and deny death in the midst of their funerals. The recollection of both of these deaths occurs while Haze is on the train for Taulkinham in flight from Eastrod, sleeping fitfully in an upper berth which "In his half sleep he thought . . . was like a coffin" (p. 19). Waking up in panic and seeing the porter, Haze calls upon Jesus only to be answered sourly by the Negro, "Jesus been a long time gone" (p. 27). It is apparent, then, that Haze's violent rejection of Jesus arises from his literal hope for immediate physical resurrection in this world and his subsequent sense of betrayal when his hope is shattered.

Once he leaves Eastrod, Haze begins an almost systematic program of spiteful blasphemy against what he considers to be the source of his injury. Apropos of nothing, he tells a strange woman on the train that he does not believe in Jesus and would not "even if He existed. Even if He was on this train" (p. 16). In Taulkinham he patronizes Mrs. Leora Watts, the prostitute, to prove through action that he does not believe in sin; and he buys a car, a dilapidated Essex, as a defiant replacement for his soul, contending that "Nobody with a good car needs to be justified" (p. 113). The Essex becomes for him the rock of his gospel from which he disseminates the truth of his Church Without Christ. He preaches the doctrines of nothingness from the car with as much vigor and threatening directness as Haze's grandfather had summoned in Christ's name, and the young prophet's conviction is borne out in his burdenlike profession, sometimes capitalized, "I am clean." Thus Haze's rejection of innate corruption through Adam, mortal sin of any kind, and the total scheme of Christian redemption becomes apparent.

Nevertheless, Haze is subconsciously driven to regain his lost faith. His hope is apparent not only in the fact that he protests too much, but in his fascination with the hypocritical pseudo-blind preacher Asa Hawks. His interest in Hawks's blindness is thematically similar to Mrs. Flood's curiosity about Haze's blindness later in the novel; Haze suspects that the old man is not blind, but he paradoxically entertains the hope that someone has had faith enough to choose inward vision in preference to outward sight. Thus the discovery that Hawks is not blind renews Haze's commitment to evil and impels him to succumb to the corruption of Sabbath Lily Hawks.

For this grotesque saint, submission to Sabbath Lily is a dark night of the soul. Haze emerges from the experience with his eyes burned clean enough to see through the fraudulence around him and with his will strengthened sufficiently to act decisively in carrying out his still-blasphemous, but sternly moral, beliefs. His first act is the destruction of the new jesus—the mummified shrunken man brought by Enoch Emery and coddled like a living child by Sabbath. Haze proves here his earlier contention that the new jesus is a metaphor, not an objective thing; in this acknowledgment one can discern intellectual progress beyond his previous literal-mindedness (although one should be cautious to avoid attributing to Flannery O'Connor any doubts as to the actuality of resurrection—to her it is not a metaphor). Hazel Motes's next significant act is to seek out and destroy Solace Layfield, his rival hired by Hoover Shoats. Layfield, the false prophet of blasphemy, is a kind of anti-antichrist who represents to Haze the lowest form of dishonesty—he claims not to believe in Jesus when he actually does. Haze murders Solace by running him down repeatedly with the Essex, suggesting allegorically an action of his perverse new soul.

After the murder, Haze decides to leave Taulkinham, go to another city, and make a new beginning with the Church Without Christ. Preparing the Essex for the trip, Hazel amazes the mechanic with his doctrines, relating the car's dilapidated condition to his own spiritual condition. Five miles into the country, a patrolman stops him and genially and methodically pushes the car over an embankment, thus committing Hazel's symbolic soul to a grotesque, red-clay grave, presided over by a hunch-shouldered buzzard.

The change in Haze on this occasion is very subtly conveyed. To the policeman's questions, he replies only that he was not going anywhere anyway; in the thematic context, he is admitting that *nothing* is *nowhere,* that the Church Without Christ is a spiritual cul-de-sac. His epiphany is not marked by a vision or a suddenly violent and revelatory experience; he knows the meaning of the destroyed car, returns to town on foot, buys a bucket and a sack of quicklime. Undramatically he answers Mrs. Flood's question about his intention: " 'Blind myself,' he said and went on in the house" (p. 210). To the casual reader, Hazel Motes's blinding of himself might be interpreted as an act of despair rather than faith; such a reader would probably make the same mistake about Oedipus. But the novel denies such misreading in its detailed account of Haze's humble acts of contrite mortification, in his explicit acceptance of the Christian scheme by altering his previous refrain to "I'm not clean" (p. 224), and in the conversion of Mrs. Flood effected by his example. Finally, in "The Author's Note to the Second Edition," Flannery O'Connor herself explains Haze as "a Christian *malgre lui*":

That belief in Christ is to some a matter of life and death as been a stumbling block for readers who would prefer to think it a matter of no great consequence. For them Hazel Motes' integrity lies in his trying with such vigor to get rid of the ragged figure who moves from tree to tree in the back of his mind. For the author Hazel's integrity lies in his not being able to.[10]

The character of Francis Marion Tarwater has already been touched upon in the analyses of other characters in *The Violent Bear It Away*—Bishop, the stranger, Rayber, and Mason Tarwater. Like Hazel Motes, young Tarwater rebels against the Christian life thrust upon him by his great-uncle. At fourteen, Tarwater has lost to death his Christian mentor. Now at the

10. Flannery O'Connor, "Author's Note to the Second Edition," *Wise Blood,* p. 5.

age of confirmation, Tarwater must decide for himself whether to accept or reject his role as baptizer and prophet—a choice which also indicates his acceptance or rejection of grace. He does not take this issue lightly at any point in the novel; the depth and strong fiber of his character are revealed in his frequent acknowledgment that he must declare his identity with God or against Him through acts and not merely through profession. He refuses to be led into a false dilemma by the stranger's voice, knowing that his choice is between Jesus and the Devil, not between Jesus and himself. He states his commitment to action when he considers drowning Bishop:

"You can't just say NO," he said. "You got to show it. You got to show you mean it by doing it. You got to show you're not going to do one thing by doing another. You got to make an end of it. One way or another" (*Violent*, p. 157).

It is Tarwater's insistence upon performance pursuant to belief that causes him to reject his uncle Rayber; Tarwater wants to accept Rayber's agnosticism, but he is scornful of his uncle's inability to carry out its humanistic imperative in regard to murdering Bishop mercifully.

Of course, Tarwater finally accomplishes Bishop's death and simultaneous baptism, but in spite of all his devotion to acting out his convictions, through most of the novel he is incapable of it himself. Yet from the beginning he knows quite well what decision he should make; when old Mason speaks to him of his own decisiveness in bringing the boy to Powderhead, Tarwater "would move his thin shoulder blades irritably as if he were shifting the burden of Truth like a cross on his back" (p. 79) .

Tarwater's indecision and his susceptibility to the error Rayber and the voice recommend have their origin in his immaturity and lack of experience. The two most reprehensible acts in his early life are his getting drunk on the day of his great-uncle's death and burning the house at Powderhead, believing it to contain old Mason's corpse. The first is an act of adolescent escapism, while the second, though a virtual failure in its blasphemous intent, is an act of which he is nervously proud. For the most part, however, he knows evil only intellectually until he drowns Bishop and is violated by the homosexual. Just as Hazel Motes finally recognizes that he is not clean and subsequently becomes a grotesque saint, Tarwater sees that he has been made unclean, acknowledges his fallen nature, and with this matured conception of himself accepts God's mercy.

Several patterns of imagery thematically associated with the action indicate Tarwater's rough progress toward epiphany. Fire, for example, is Tarwater's mode of defiance in the burning of Powderhead; his great-uncle, however, has spoken to him of the divine significance of fire in describing the burning effect of God's mercy and of a prophet's ministry. And so it is with- Tarwater after his violation; when he awakens from the effects of the drugged whiskey, "His eyes looked small and seedlike as if while he was asleep, they had been lifted out, scorched, and dropped back into his head" (p. 232) . After his eyes are thus burned clean, he uses fire to purify the contaminated ground and later to dispel the presence of the devil's voice; finally he hears, as he had hoped to earlier, the voice of the Lord commanding him from a burning tree at Powderhead: "He knew that this was the fire that had encircled Daniel, that had raised Elijah from the earth, that had spoken to Moses and would in the instant speak to him" (p. 242).

A similar pattern appears in images relating to clothes, the city, water, and food; they show a movement from Tarwater's rejection of the efficacious significance of the images in the beginning and middle of the novel to his ultimate acceptance of their sacramental import in the conclusion. He abandons his self-conscious fetishes about clothes; he turns toward the city, not as an escape from the old prophet's influence, but in obedience to him and God; he uses water—almost against his will—to baptize Bishop; and his persistent hunger and inability to eat are resolved by the vision which comes to him as he watches Buford Munson disappear across the corn field:

The boy remained standing there, his still eyes reflecting the field the Negro had crossed. It seemed to him no longer empty but peopled with a multitude. Everywhere, he saw dim figures seated on the slope and as he gazed he saw that from a single basket the throng was being fed. His eyes searched the crowd for a long time as if he could not find the one he was looking for. Then he saw him. The old man was lowering himself to the ground. When he was down and his bulk had settled, he leaned forward, his face turned toward the basket, impatiently following its progress toward him. The boy too leaned forward, aware at last of the object of his hunger, aware that it was the same as the old man's and that nothing on earth would fill him. His hunger was so great that he could have eaten all the loaves and fishes after they were multiplied (*Violent*, p. 241).

This is a vision of heaven in which Tarwater sees the fulfillment of one of the Beatitudes, "Blessed are they which do hunger and thirst after righteousness: for they shall be filled" (Matt. 5:6). Christ's pronouncement is, of course, merged with the accounts of His miraculous feeding of the multitude, each serving as a gloss upon the other and signifying in the novel the righteousness of both Tarwater and his great-uncle, their dissatisfaction with merely earthly sustenance, and their reward in heaven for accepting God's grace and following His call. In the light of such passages, it is difficult to understand why some critics have taken *The Violent Bear It Away* as a novel of despair; indeed, the boy's vision is described to illustrate the opposite—that he has won his struggle with the powers of inner darkness.

Visions also climax the struggle with spiritual pride in the major characters of "The Enduring Chill" and "Revelation." Asbury Fox is sternly admonished by Father Finn, the priest whose orthodoxy disappoints the young boy. Father Finn correctly refers to him as an ignorant youth, and finally Asbury's agnosticism, intellectual superiority, and self-righteous liberalism succumb to the implacable descent of the Holy Ghost. His acceptance of grace takes him by surprise, for in the extremity of his fear of death, he is unaware that his own will has become inclined to God. Upon learning from Dr. Block that he has been spared the death he pretended romantically to relish but which actually terrified him, he sees in the bedroom mirror that his eyes, like those of so many other O'Connor characters, have been burned clean by the experience and thus prepared for the imminent vision: a peculiar chill overtakes him

and the bird outlined by water stains over his bed
appears to move. "The Holy Ghost, emblazoned in ice
instead of fire, continued, implacable, to descend" (*Everything,* p. 114).

Mrs. Turpin, in "Revelation," is not an evil woman;
she is good and hardworking, "not so far gone in pride
as the Mrs. McIntyres and the Mrs. Mays."[11] Although
Mary Grace's epithet (an "old wart hog from hell")
may be shocking and extreme, Mrs. Turpin is nevertheless guilty of appalling satisfaction with herself,
whereas the Wellesley girl at least knows that she is
ugly and cannot live with the fact. In thanking God
that she is who she is, Mrs. Turpin erroneously attributes her expected salvation to her personal identity
rather than to her convergent identity in Christ, which
entails the loss of the self. As Robert Drake points out
generally about Flannery O'Connor's view, "There is,
finally, no salvation in *works,* whatever form they may
take, or in *self.*"[12] After an entire day of puzzling over
the meaning of the attack upon her in the doctor's
office, Mrs. Turpin is enlightened by a vision which
comes, ironically as she stands in the immaculate pig
parlor, spraying the animals with water to cleanse them
and looking outside toward the sunset. In the evening
sky she sees that she and Claud are among the saved
derelicts such as she saw in the doctor's office, but that
she and her husband are there only because their virtues, and thus their pride, are being burned away.

Calhoun and Mary Elizabeth in "The Partridge Festival" also suffer from self-satisfaction, with their pride
taking the form of smart-aleck liberalism. Both of them

11. Robert Drake, *Flannery O'Connor: A Critical Essay,* p. 29.
12. *Ibid.,* p. 36.

blame the commercialism of the people of Partridge
when an insane man, Singleton, murders six of the
town's leading citizens at the inauguration of the local
azalea festival. Serious college students, both Calhoun
and Mary Elizabeth consider Singleton a scapegoat, a
local Christ unjustly committed to an insane asylum.
Calhoun avowedly repudiates the values of his parents,
unaware that his own inexplicable love of selling elec-
trical appliances is the sign of his essential kinship in
spirit as well as in blood with his grandfather, the foun-
der of the annual commercialized celebration of
beauty; "Beauty is Our Money Crop,"[13] said the grandfather, and Calhoun claims, "They prostitute azaleas"
("Festival," p. 382).

They sat silently, looking at nothing until finally they
turned and looked at each other. There each saw at once
the likeness of their kinsman and flinched. They looked
away and then back, as if with concentration they might
find a more tolerable image. To Calhoun, the girl's face
seemed to mirror the nakedness of the sky. In despair he
leaned closer until he was stopped by a miniature visage
which rose incorrigibly in her spectacles and fixed him
where he was. Round, innocent, undistinguished as an iron
link, it was the face whose gift of life had pushed straight
forward to the future to raise festival after festival. Like a
master salesman, it seemed to have been waiting there from
all time to claim him ("Festival," pp. 389–390).

Both the boy and the girl discover that there are no easy
answers to human behavior—that the sociologist's ab-
stractions and the novelist's thematic generalities often

13. Flannery O'Connor, "The Partridge Festival," reprinted in
The Sense of Fiction, Welker and Gower, editors, p. 376. Further
quotations from this work will be identified with the abbreviation
"Festival" and a page number in parentheses.

fail to convey the complexity of a situation. They realize that Singleton is guilty but not responsible; that Partridge is right about him but not innocent; and that they themselves had seen the mote in their brother's eye without considering the beam in theirs. Finally they perceive the incredibly complex mystery of existence that, when known, purges one of pride and fosters humility.

Like Calhoun and Mary Elizabeth, Julian in "Everything That Rises Must Converge" is intelligent and considers himself more broad-minded than his mother. Cynical and misanthropic, he is unable to find a suitable job even though he has been out of college for a year; he has no charity, no love, and no sympathy for his mother, who has done everything for him. Like the characters in "The Partridge Festival" he scoffs at his mother's values, even though he secretly knows the truth of her contention that one's identity is rooted in the past and the family traditions that have been lost; he dreams of the decayed mansion that had once been the family's home, but his pride permits him to feel that his mother could not appreciate its meaning as well as he. The epiphany which shatters the insularity of his mocking interior life is effected when Julian creates a situation that he thinks will teach his mother a lesson in racial tolerance. The lesson is Julian's, when he learns that the attack upon his mother by the Negro woman whose child she has patronized brings on a fatal stroke. Knowing personal responsibility for the first time, Julian calls upon his mother tenderly but futilely and in that moment crosses over into maturity and knowledge. Imploring his stricken mother to wait, he runs toward a cluster of lights, calling for help and realizing the imminence of guilt.

The final character among those who are clearly in acceptance of grace after having lived insensitive to it is O. E. Parker, the tattooed man in "Parker's Back." Parker's tattoos symbolize not only his vanity but his lifelong commitment to secular experiences which have no sustaining significance; he becomes quickly dissatisfied with each tattoo and perceives that their total effect is "haphazard and botched" (p. 224). He wishes to emulate the tattooed man who had inspired him as a youth, filling him with an admiration and reverence typical of religious experiences:

Parker had never before felt the least motion of wonder in himself. Until he saw the man at the fair, it did not enter his head that there was anything out of the ordinary about the fact that he existed. Even then it did not enter his head, but a peculiar unease settled in him. It was as if a blind boy had been turned so gently in a different direction that he did not know his destination had been changed (p. 223).

Parker's destiny is manifest when he submits himself to carrying the image of Christ on his back, realizing finally that, like the other tattooed man, his existence might thus inspire others. This point is verified by the significance of the allusion to Elihu, the Old Testament prophet for whom Parker is named. God's truth has come to Parker from the burning tree in the field where he plowed, and he obeys the mandate given to him in that epiphany.

A small group of characters to whom grace is offered may be distinguished from those just examined in that they recognize the opportunity for grace only at the moment of violent death, with the result that one is left uncertain as to their acceptance or rejection of it. This difficulty of interpretation can be overcome, however, if one applies to it the notion inherent in the title of Flannery O'Connor's last collection of stories, that salvation proceeds from rising, however slightly, towards God. In *Wise Blood*, for example, Solace Layfield denies God in word and deed by posing as the prophet of the Church Without Christ, but his last words to his executioner, Hazel Motes, are those of confession and devoutness, and they are sufficient proof against damnation. The grandmother in "A Good Man Is Hard to Find" is not as specifically evil as Solace Layfield, but she does fail to acknowledge her identity with fallen man at large, believing in a limited and ill-conceived community of good country people. As the Misfit says about her, "She would of been a good woman . . . if it had been somebody there to shoot her every minute of her life" (*Good Man*, p. 29). But like the rest of her family, she is shallow, vulgar, selfish, and generally unattractive. They are a family of the mildly damned— damned not because they are evil, but because they have never seen deeply enough into an experience to be aware that damnation is a possibility or that salvation is an issue. The story, however, is not the family's but the grandmother's; it is she whose epiphany gives the story its thematic center. Having spent her life mouthing facile platitudes such as that of the story's title, she is brought dramatically to a juncture at which she realizes the inadequacy of her former beliefs. Flannery O'Connor describes the significance of the confrontation between the Grandmother and the Misfit:

There is a moment of grace in most of the stories, or a moment where it is offered, and is usually rejected. Like when the Grandmother recognizes the Misfit as one of her own children and reaches out to touch him. It's the moment of grace for her anyway—a silly old woman—but it leads him to shoot her. This moment of grace excites the devil to frenzy.[14]

The words of the grandmother's acceptance of grace are her last, and they are words of mercy, compassion, and Christian vision: "Why you're one of my babies. You're one of my own children."

An equally violent death is suffered by Mary Fortune Pitts in "A View of the Woods." The child is a harridan who mirrors the bad qualities of her grandfather, ironically turning them upon him when he stubbornly sells the piece of land that she cherishes. In astonishingly violent fits of temper, she and the old man kill each other. Sister Bertrande, in a perceptive analysis of this story, finds the redemptive feature of the child's behavior in the fact that she brings about her family's inheritance of the land in question through her death and the grandfather's; her role is thus comparable to that of Moses leading the children of Israel into the Promised Land. "It might be added," she says, "that death, in spite of its needless violence, was for her a distinctive redemptive grace. What she might have become a few years more under the devastating tutelage of old Mark Fortune is unpleasant and unnecessary to contemplate."[15]

14. Letter from Flannery O'Connor to Andrew Lytle, February 4, 1960, Tennessee State Library and Archives, Nashville, Tennessee.

15. "Four Stories of Flannery O'Connor," *Thought*, XXVII (Autumn 1962), 424.

Mrs. May, who dies on the ragged horns of a scrub bull, also undergoes a violent epiphany. She is similar to Mrs. McIntyre in "The Displaced Person" because she is not religious but practical; her chief interest is to wrest a profit from her dairy farm, and her main regret arises from her proud disappointment that her two sons have—to her way of thinking—failed by comparison with the twin sons of her hired man, Mr. Greenleaf. She undergoes no spiritual struggles in the story, only shallow secular ones, but the moment of her death seems to suggest that such violence was necessary to effect the small insight needed for rising and convergence. After the bull gores her, burying its head in her lap "like a wild tormented lover," Mrs. May's expression changes:

She continued to stare straight ahead but the entire scene in front of her had changed—the tree line was a dark wound in a world that was nothing but sky—and she had the look of a person whose sight has been suddenly restored but who finds the light unbearable (*Everything*, p. 52).

As she dies, Mr. Greenleaf, who has killed the bull, notices "that she . . . seemed to be bent over whispering some last discovery into the animal's ear" (p. 53).

It seems apparent, then, that Flannery O'Connor wishes to identify those who achieve Christian redemption. Whether she indicates it through direct statement, by the objective actions of characters, by visions, or by subtle revelation of an interior condition, she leaves little question that she means for her readers to apprehend the moment of grace as surely as her characters do.

Chapter 5 Symbols of Spiritual Reality

THE insistent presence of the religious theme in nearly all of Flannery O'Connor's fiction indicates that from her sacramental point of view all human action is relevant to spiritual realities, whether the action is or is not sympathetic with Christian or religious values. She sees actions that are not even denials of religious meanings in her own special Christian context. To this extent all of her fiction is symbolic, in that the actions of her characters are plausible and understandable on the naturalistic plane and yet take their final meanings from a plane above the natural. She says that "A Good Man Is Hard to Find" is naturalistic writing,[1] and yet she explains elsewhere that the story is the representation of the Grandmother's recognition and acceptance of grace. Similarly, in "Judgement Day," old Tanner's struggle is a physical

---

1. Flannery O'Connor, "A Collection of Statements," compiled by Lewis A. Lawson, *The Added Dimension: The Art and Mind of Flannery O'Connor,* edited by Melvin J. Friedman and Lewis A. Lawson, p. 258.

one, but the reader cannot miss the significance of this action as spiritual, a movement toward salvation and resurrection. In varying degrees all of her stories symbolically represent the dramatization of a spiritual journey of the soul. Such cosmic action is one form of symbolism in her fiction.

But her habit of mind led her so commonly to see through the naturalistic plane of action to the spiritual that the natural fused effortlessly with the spiritual; consequently, she did not think of this dimension of her fiction as symbolic. In a panel discussion at Wesleyan College she claimed, in her characteristically dry manner, not to have known what symbols were until she started reading about them.[2] Her comments there and elsewhere and her fictional practice indicate that she thought of symbolism not as a pervasive level of meaning but as a limited device which could focus and emphasize the meaning of a story or novel. She says that "a symbol is sort of like the engine in a story"—an object, image, or action which is "turning or working the story." On one occasion she cites Hulga Hopewell's wooden leg as an example of the use of symbolism in her stories, and she adds to the example a definition of symbolism which accurately reflects her technique: "Symbols are big things that knock you in the face."[3]

Although some of her symbols are traditional Christian ones, she does not jeopardize their meanings with subtlety. In "The Displaced Person," for example, the ubiquity of the peacock is notable; whether or not one is aware that the peacock is a traditional symbol of

2. *Ibid.*, p. 259.
3. *Ibid.*

Christ, specifically associated with Holy Communion, the Christian meaning soon becomes apparent to him through the repetition of the symbol in sympathetic association with the priest, Astor, and Mr. Guizac, and through Mrs. McIntyre's hostility towards the peacock.

Although the peacock is mentioned briefly and used fleetingly in a symbolic way, nowhere else is it used extensively. But another significant example of traditional symbolism occurs in "The Enduring Chill." In this story, stains on the wall above the dying Asbury's bed resemble a descending bird with an icicle in its beak and icicles depending from its wings. The bird is not specifically referred to as a dove, but a suggestive connection is drawn by the priest who tells the boy that he should ask God to send him the Holy Ghost. More specifically, at the end of the story when Asbury learns that he is not dying, he has a vision of the inevitability of his own salvation, signaled by a red-gold sun moving from under a cloud and by the fierce bird's descent. The bird in this final appearance in the story is described specifically as "the Holy Ghost, emblazoned in ice instead of fire."[4]

When considering such symbolism as occurs in these two stories, one could object that the author is deficient in technique to the extent that she clearly identifies the meaning of the symbols. But in both instances the recognition of the meaning comes from a character in the story, not from authorial comment. It is perfectly natural that the priest in "The Displaced Person" makes the

4. Flannery O'Connor, *Everything That Rises Must Converge,* p. 114. Further quotations from this work will be identified with the abbreviation *Everything* and a page number in parentheses.

equation between the peacock and Christ. In "The Enduring Chill" Asbury's mind has been bound up with
religious questions throughout the story; he has been
admonished by the old priest concerning the Holy
Ghost; and in the end, his epiphany is objectified in his
own mind (through the limited point of view) and not
by the author's authority. The degree of explicitness
regarding symbols may vary from one story to the next,
but in general, O'Connor's practice is to nail down her
meaning quite clearly, not relying absolutely upon traditional significance or emergent significance by association.

Just as O'Connor's characters are drawn large and
unmistakable and yet are believable, so are her symbols.
The burning bush as the source of God's voice or God's
imperative to man occurs in "Parker's Back." Its significance is pointed out, but one's critical sensibilities are
not offended by the manner in which the identification
of the symbol is made; it is prepared for and is a natural
outcome of the character of O. E. Parker—his mind and
his method of expressing himself. Parker's first words in
the story are a series of oaths: " 'God dammit!' he hol-
lered, 'Jesus Christ in hell! Jesus God Almighty damn!
God dammit to hell!' " (*Everything*, p. 221) His words
at this point are nothing more than oaths, but a tissue
of meaning begins to establish itself immediately when
Sarah Ruth, the girl he eventually marries, is described
as a "giant hawk-eyed angel"; she subsequently becomes
a harpy for God to her husband. Later, when he crashes
his tractor into a tree, it is perfectly natural for him to
yell, "GOD ABOVE!" His outcry has changed from blas-

phemous oath to awed recognition, its emphasis from hell to heaven. As the ignited tree burns, his wife's lessons coalesce with his own words to reveal the tree's symbolic meaning to him and to the reader at the same time. In the light of such developments, there can be no objection to the author's comment that" if he had known how to cross himself he would have done it" (p. 233). The success of this symbol prepares the way for the even more explicit symbol of Parker's having the image of a Byzantine Christ tattooed on his back.

The symbolism of fire is not, even in the case of O. E. Parker, limited to signifying the presence of God; the fire ignited by O. E.'s tractor is purgatorial too, for it symbolically consumes O. E.'s former identity when it burns his shoes, causing him to go barefoot into town to have Christ tatooed on his back. In *The Violent Bear It Away*, Tarwater tries to purge his spiritual identity in the beginning of the novel by burning the body of his grandfather in the house at Powderhead; but this perversity in him is finally repudiated in the end of the novel, the symbol of the change being the fire which he uses to purge the ground where he was criminally violated and symbolically spoiled. With fire he exorcises the devil which pursues him back to his original home, spiritual and circumstantial. Such complexity of the use of the fire symbol is apparent in much of O'Connor's fiction, but its most obvious manifestation other than in "Parker's Back" and *The Violent Bear It Away* is in "A Circle in the Fire," in which the boys' malicious use of fire provides Mrs. Cope with the opportunity to be burned clean of her lack of charity. Not chastened, she fails to see that God has flared before her in the image of violence; all she sees is the fire.

In *The Violent Bear It Away*, fire is only one of many symbols; but one pair of symbols—water and food in their symbolic function relating to baptism and the Eucharist—may be understood to be the engine of the novel. Old Tarwater's injunction to his nephew is to carry out the baptism of the idiot child Bishop Rayber; on several different occasions Bishop is attracted to water in the park, thus demonstrating his affinity for water and therefore for baptism. In these scenes there can be no doubt as to the significance of his yearning for water; the symbolism is not tortured and self-conscious, but neither is it coy or obscure. These scenes represent the high points in the novel in that they most dramatically objectify the conflict within Tarwater and point out the theme of the novel. The baptism-murder of Bishop is also obvious in its relevance to the sacrament of baptism for Bishop; and yet the symbol remains vital in the ambiguity of the event in regard to the character of Tarwater. One is left wondering whether or not his action partakes of salvation or damnation.

The resolution of this question is forthcoming through the appearance of the other of this pair of symbols. Throughout the novel, Tarwater is hungry or preoccupied with food; quite early in the action the description of his uncle's eyes as fishlike associates him with Christ's feeding of the multitude. Tarwater himself finally rejects worldly food and is treated to a vision of Christ feeding the multitude when he realizes that he is after all spiritually one with his uncle and with God.

Miss O'Connor does not rely exclusively upon traditional Christian symbolism. In "Good Country People," for example, a woman's soul is symbolized, unlikely as it may seem, by her artificial leg. When Hulga Hopewell is said to be as sensitive about it as a peacock is of his tail, the association with this traditional Christian symbol is significant; further, she takes care of it "as someone else would his soul,"[5] and Manley Pointer, the Bible salesman, tells Hulga reverently that the leg is what makes her different from other people. Although the symbolism is obvious, it is not simple. Hulga's loss of her real leg when she was only ten years old was a traumatic experience which led directly to her sense of despair and her renunciation of God and her own former unquestioning self, symbolized by the change in her name from Joy to Hulga. Subsequently the artificial leg became for her an object other than her body, yet an intimate part of her, as the soul is. Yet she is contemptuous of the artificial leg as she is of the notion of the soul. When she learns the full physical value of the leg, she also learns that her philosophy has stolen away her soul as Manley Pointer has carried away her leg.

Shocking symbolism is usual rather than extraordinary throughout Miss O'Connor's work; in "The Lame Shall Enter First" physical deformity is again the engine that makes the story work. The characters in this story resemble those in *The Violent Bear It Away;* Sheppard, a social worker and a widower, neglects his own son Norton and devotes his love and attention to

5. Flannery O'Connor, *A Good Man Is Hard to Find,* p. 192. Further quotations from this work will be identified with the abbreviation *Good Man* and a page number in parentheses.

Rufus Johnson, a bright, religiously fanatical juvenile delinquent who condescendingly accepts Sheppard's favors but correctly mocks him as a tin Jesus and a moral leper. The extent of Sheppard's perverse charity is apparent in his repeated defense of Rufus when the boy is guilty of willful and gratuitous vandalism and voyeurism. When Sheppard attempts to broaden the boy's mind by allowing him to use a microscope and telescope, Rufus is unmoved and turns such knowledge upon Sheppard by explaining to Norton the Christian concepts of heaven and immortality, thus arousing in the child the hope, assiduously denied by his father, that he will be able to see his dead mother again. Rufus's grotesqueness is not only a matter of his social and religious intractability, but is physically apparent in his deformity, a monstrous, extraordinarily ugly clubfoot. The symbolism here is quite similar to that of Hulga's leg, in that both indicate paradoxically that the soul is not moribund but is dark and ugly. Sheppard attributes Rufus's incorrigibility to compensation for the foot, whereas the reader takes the deformity to indicate moral depravity. Rufus acknowledges this depravity, saying that Satan "has me in his power" (*Everything,* p. 150), and he relishes the sign of it by using the clubfoot as a weapon and by steadfastly refusing to allow it to be palliated by an orthopedic shoe. When Sheppard takes him to the brace shop to be measured for the appliance, Rufus is "touchy about the foot as if it were a sacred object" (p. 162). There is a preternatural aptness in the fact that the first shoe made for him inexplicably will not fit even though careful measurements have been taken. The second fitting is correct, but Rufus refuses to wear the shoe. The scene is one of the ugliest in Flannery O'Connor's stories:

> The brace shop was a small concrete warehouse lined and stacked with the equipment of affliction. Wheel chairs and walkers covered most of the floor. The walls were hung with every kind of crutch and brace. Artificial limbs were stacked on the shelves, legs and arms and hands, claws and hooks, straps and human harnesses and unidentifiable instruments for unnamed deformities. In a small clearing in the middle of the room there was a row of yellow plastic-cushioned chairs and a shoe fitting stool. Johnson slouched down in one of the chairs and set his foot up on the stool and sat with his eyes on it moodily. What was roughly the toe had broken open again and he had patched it with a piece of canvas; another place he had patched with what appeared to be the tongue of the original shoe. The two sides were laced with twine (*Everything,* p. 175).

The new shoe looks "like a blunt weapon, highly polished," and the clerk removes the old one "as if he were skinning an animal still half alive" (p. 175).

The critical question raised by this scene is whether its extremity is needed for thematic purposes. Its grotesqueness exists not so much in the event itself as in the visual rendering of it; in this respect it goes far beyond other actions that are essentially more grotesque, such as Hazel Motes's blinding of himself and Tarwater's drowning of Bishop, both thematically profound and yet visually underplayed. Certainly the full meaning of the symbol of Rufus Johnson's deliberate depravity is achieved most effectively through this scene, but its visual impact is less important to this end than the boy's refusal to wear the shoe. One must conclude, then, that the visual extremity is not gratuitous only on the grounds that Flannery O'Connor refuses to soften the reality of an unpleasant scene that is dramatically necessary to the action. To play down this scene would be to take the risk of enlisting false sympathy for a deformed person, and this is an artistic risk which has no place in the actions of Hazel Motes and Tarwater. She means to allow no misinterpretation of the title of the story; the lame do not enter heaven first because they are the object of divine sentiment for crippled children, but because spiritual lameness like Rufus Johnson's, if it is acknowledged, calls forth the greatest rejoicing in heaven and the most profound mercy of God. This is the import of the parable of the prodigal son: it is because the spiritually corrupt son has reformed that he is feted by the father, not because he became a profligate. The spiritually deformed enter heaven first only because they have genuinely accepted salvation and grace, not because they may be incidentally lame. The grotesqueness of the scene from "The Lame Shall Enter First" leaves no doubt that Rufus's grotesque condition is spiritual as well as physical. Only through genuine salvation shall the lame enter heaven at all, not because they are afflicted. That Rufus may be one of the actual lame so saved along with the spiritually lame such as Sheppard, who undergo epiphanies, is indicated when Johnson in the height of his depravity, accusing Sheppard of immoral advances, is said to be "on the threshold of some dark apocalypse" (p. 185) .

Outlandish symbols for the soul find parallels in equally unusual symbols for God, or more precisely, certain divine functions in the phenomenal world—the sort of symbolism that takes conventional forms such as the peacock or the icy bird in "The Enduring Chill." "Greenleaf" is constructed around the story's symbol of God, a scrub bull which metaphorically stands for God as surely as Zeus is himself when he appears to Europa in the same form. Mrs. May, the protagonist of the story, is one of O'Connor's practical people, a believer in salvation through works. Like her socially inferior counterpart in the story, Mrs. Greenleaf (who indulges in grotesque prayer healing and is preoccupied with the revolting sufferings depicted in yellow journalism), Mrs. May is obsessed with the evil and unjust nature of the world, specifically the superiority of the hired man Greenleaf's children to her own and, more immediately, the Greenleaf twins' bull which is contaminating her own herd and ruining her yard and fences. The bull represents the injustices of her life, the indignities which she has suffered. Being killed by it at the end of the story is the final indignity suffered at the hands of the Greenleafs of the world, but it is also the indignity which opens her eyes to the nature of the world—the realization that what she construes as injustice is a part of the scheme God has prepared for man and part of the inheritance of fallen man. Ironically she thinks that there is a fitting justice in Mr. Greenleaf's having to shoot his own sons' bull; one realizes that if justice is to be served, Mrs. May must suffer as surely as the shiftless and proud Mr. Greenleaf does. On the basis of the symbolism of the bull, it appears that Mrs. May's epiphany as she dies on the bull's horns is associated with the question of justice—her recognition of its inevitability.

The bull, then, symbolizes the justice of God in its destructiveness and the love of Christ in its function of saving Mrs. May by revealing the truth to her.

A polarity comparable to that found in the symbol of the bull is apparent in the prevailing symbol indicated by the very title, "The Artificial Nigger." Although the plaster statue itself does not appear until the conclusion, it is nevertheless the engine that makes the story work by merit of the title and the insistent pattern of imagery that anticipates the symbol—blackness of the night, darkness of the labyrinthine sewer of Atlanta, the Negro on the train, and the seemingly inimical Negroes of the city's ghetto in which Nelson and Mr. Head become lost. All of these images finally become involved in the blackness of the artificial Negro; and light finally arises from darkness, mercy from suffering.

A metaphor for the action of "The Artificial Nigger" is provided in an allusion to Dante's *Divine Comedy*, the comparison between Mr. Head and Vergil as Dante's guide to the Inferno suggesting that the voyage of the old man and his grandson is analogous to an epic descent into the underworld. Even the preparations of the two countrymen to leave are pervaded by a surrealistic confounding of reality; when Mr. Head awakens in the night before they leave, the humble room is flooded with moonlight that transforms the rustic floor to the color of silver, the pillow ticking to brocade; the moon itself comes into the room through reflection in a shaving mirror. Even the chair and Mr. Head's clothes draped on it are transformed to items of heroic dignity, and the slop jar near Nelson "appears to stand guard over him like a small personal angel" (*Good Man,* p. 103).

Once they leave home, the surrealistic imagery is no longer ameliorative but presents ordinary objects in a terrifying manner. When they arrive at the railroad junction, a coarse, orange, rising sun turns the beautiful moon gray and transparent, "hardly stronger than a thumbprint and completely without light" (p. 106). Trains emerge from a dark tunnel of trees and "hit for a second by the cold sky, vanish terrified into the woods again" (p. 106). When their train arrives, its horn is a "warning bleat" and the conductor has "the face of an ancient bloated bulldog" (p. 107). Inside the train, their reflections in the window are pale and ghostlike, and Mr. Head's attempts to ingratiate himself to the passengers are ludicrous and do more to alienate them and to transform him and his grandson into things than to increase their humanity. Arriving in Atlanta, they gaze through their own reflections at an endless series of advertisements, as amazed by these banalities as if they were the ciphers of salvation and not the pointers to the underworld. The conductor's announcement of the first stop, Emory, becomes to their displaced ears, "Firstopppppmry" (p. 113).

Their first actual mistake is leaving their paper sack of lunch on the train, symbolizing their separation in the underworld from the saving strength of the Eucharist—their abandonment of their true country for a landscape so unfamiliar to them that it takes on the aspect of a nightmare and hell itself. They marvel at the entrances of stores but refuse to enter them for fear of becoming lost, as Mr. Head was on his one previous visit to Atlanta. Both of them are constantly aware of this threat, which is made concrete by several references to the labyrinthine city sewer. Mr. Head explains the terrors of "endless pitchblack tunnels" while the shaken Nelson stoops and listens, associating "the sewer passages with the entrance to hell" (p. 116).

When they actually become lost, they find themselves amid Negroes, to them dark and mysterious exotics. Nelson's mad dash when Mr. Head tricks him leads subsequently to a hellish press of people accusing Nelson and sneering at Mr. Head's denial of his own flesh. The old man's moral and geographical disorientation after this incident takes him "into a black strange place where nothing was like it had ever been before" (p. 125), and Nelson's attempt to preserve his indignation causes him to feel "a black mysterious form reach up as if it would melt his frozen image in one hot grasp" (p. 125). Details of this kind represent a remarkable meshing of the outward events and the underlying moral theme of the story. The voyage to the underworld ends when both characters, against the background of a darkening evening sky, recognize the meaning of the underworld's darkness, identify themselves with it as they look at the artificial Negro, and, like Dante, are miraculously able to return to their true country with this saving knowledge.

A tasteless and battered yard ornament is as unlikely an object as one may find to symbolize the presence of Christian sympathy, charity, and humility; yet the symbol is not facetious—indeed, it is profound in its combining of classical, Christian, archetypal, and local associations. Like so many of O'Connor's symbols, this one is big and insolent—on first impression, an outlandish slap in the face. Its final effect, however, is quite other-wise—almost serene. This paradoxical quality is charac-teristic of O'Connor's symbolism, as it is of her art in general.

Chapter *6* The
Gothic
Impulse

FLANNERY O'CONNOR'S
narratives are built upon situations and characters
usually beyond the experience of those whose line of
vision seldom strays from their personal views of the
normal world. Her readers and critics repeatedly call
attention to the high incidence of the grotesque, revolting, and ugly features of her settings and characters and
thus categorize her as a writer of Gothic fiction. She
herself, however, was not at all preoccupied or self-conscious about these characteristics of her work; for example, she says in a letter to Ihab Hassan, "It never occurred to me that my novel [*Wise Blood*] was grotesque
until I read it in the papers."[1]

Although she had, in public lectures and panel dis-
cussions and in the few essays she allowed to be published, addressed herself to the question of the grotesque in literature and in her own work, Miss
O'Connor was not sympathetic toward broad generali-

1. As quoted in Ihab Hassan, *Radical Innocence: Studies in
the Contemporary American Novel*, p. 79.

zations. For example, she did not approve of "Southern School of Writers" and "Southern Gothic" as terms; in Granville Hicks's symposium, *The Living Novel,* she says that the use of these terms "conjures up an image of Gothic monstrosities and the idea of a preoccupation with everything deformed and grotesque. Most of us are considered, I believe, to be unhappy combinations of Poe and Erskine Caldwell."[2] Implicit in her demur is the quite obvious fact that Gothic and grotesque are terms sufficiently broad in meaning to be more confusing than enlightening when used without qualification. Acknowledging this difficulty, at least one critic of Miss O'Connor's fiction, Sumner J. Ferris, has refused to use the terms at all, contending that "Such vogue words as 'decadent' and 'Gothic' are so vague as to be almost meaningless."[3] Even though confusion does exist, the terms clearly have meaning when correctly applied to Flannery O'Connor's work; these qualities in her work are so extensive that one cannot ignore them nor circumvent them.

Reluctance to apply the terms Gothic and grotesque, or careless misapplication of them, results from several misunderstandings. First, it is often erroneously assumed that "Gothic" identifies only that literature which seeks to shock readers gratuitously, to frighten and terrify them only for the purpose of titillation. As a matter of fact, the best Gothic fiction conveys themes which are

2. Flannery O'Connor, "The Fiction Writer and His Country," *The Living Novel: A Symposium,* edited by Granville Hicks, p. 159.

3. "The Outside and the Inside: Flannery O'Connor's *The Violent Bear It Away,*" *Critique,* III (Winter-Spring 1960), 19.

congruent with the method of terror, striking a balance between manner and thematic intent. A second mistaken notion is that grotesqueness is the equivalent of Gothicism; it is not. Grotesqueness is some deviation from an explicit or implicit norm and may reside in physical attributes, actions, or situations. It may be simply verisimilitude or rhetorical overstatement; but when its intention is to promote a feeling of revulsion or terror, it is a textural necessity in Gothic fiction, serving there as an indispensable adjunct to other characteristics promoting the same end. Many modern writers—Flannery O'Connor among them—have employed grotesqueness in the Gothic mode without using other Gothic features and without purposefully creating a totally terrifying atmosphere. While some of the recent fiction of Flannery O'Connor and others like her does achieve truly Gothic proportions, a larger amount of their work reveals what may be termed the Gothic impulse—the use of grotesqueness for the purpose of arousing terror but not sustaining this atmosphere throughout nor using it as an end in itself. Thus, when the ugly and distorted are not used as literary adornment, the grotesque becomes a thematic contribution to the narrative, whether or not the story is Gothic.

The historical backgrounds of the Gothic tradition are familiar enough to preclude summary, but the examples of Gothic fiction are not homogeneous. From the time of Horace Walpole, Gothic novels and stories have ranged from shallow sensationalism to profound terror, from amateurish psychology to complex philosophy. Many critics consider Gothicism informed by serious intent the only valid literary mode of the genre, and they distinguish such fiction from the plethora of cheap, imitative journalistic practice.

Edward Wagenknecht, for example, insists that the true Gothic novel should contain *real* supernaturalism, not merely strange phenomena which science can explain as perfectly natural.[4] Devendra Varma in *The Gothic Flame* carries the point much further and puts it into a historical context. He contends that the emergence of the Gothic novel is connected with the Romantic reaction against the clockwork God of the eighteenth century, a God which stood at the center of a religion proudly rational, eschewing any form of emotionalism. Persistent, however, in the face of such a religion was man's most primitive religious instinct, his terror and awe before the power of the Divine. In the Romantic Movement, contends Varma, reaction to the reliance upon reason manifested itself partly in the phenomenon of the Gothic romance, in which he finds "a new recognition of the heart's emotions and a reassertion of the numinous."[5]

Certain strains of the new American Gothic have something in common with the earlier Gothic revival. Part of this impulse surely resides in a reaction to the sterility and extreme rationality as apparent in the twentieth century as it was in the eighteenth. Some of the contemporary writers who show a new affinity for the Gothic have reacted to the cynicism and nothingness envisioned by the writers of the earlier part of the century. They believe in spiritual truths which are difficult to communicate through characters and actions

4. *Cavalcade of the English Novel,* p. 114.
5. Pp. 210–211.

which are not unfamiliar and extraordinary. Their attempt to return to nonnaturalistic and numinous matters has, predictably, led them into fictional methods which are, like those of the earlier Gothic writers, extravagant in their distortion of the "normal" appearance of things, a distortion which is a deliberate attempt to render more accurately the character's inward nature or condition or the situation in which he has been placed. The following letter specifically indicates that Miss O'Connor's use of grotesque elements is deeply rooted in the wish to portray spiritual conditions:

But whatever Southern life may contribute to this impression of grotesquery, there is a more fundamental reason why these stories are the way they are. The reason is that the writer's vision is literal and not naturalistic. It is literal in the same sense that a child's drawing is literal. When a child draws he doesn't try to be grotesque but to set down exactly what he sees, and as his gaze is direct, he sees the lines that create motion. I am interested in the lines that create spiritual motion.[6]

But Flannery O'Connor's intention in following her impulse to the Gothic must not be interpreted as like that of current writers who take as their province the horrible, the strange, and the violent aspects of life. Thousands of subliterary writers exploit the public's appetite for sadism and gratuitous cruelty, but a more valid and interesting category of Gothic fiction includes those novels and short stories which deal in the strangeness and terror inherent in the depiction of aberrant or highly charged psychological conditions. Truman Ca-

6. As quoted by Hassan, p. 79.

pote and Carson McCullers are particularly important among the modern writers concerned with such matters, but it is essential to realize that for them Gothicism and grotesqueness are outward properties of the fiction and do not entail thematic congruency with other Gothic works. Gothicism is generic, not thematic; and yet some critics take outward Gothic qualities as sufficient reason to lump together writers of great dissimilarity. In an article on *Wise Blood,* Caroline Gordon takes issue with critics who maintain that it is impossible to tell the difference between stories by Flannery O'Connor, Carson McCullers, Tennessee Williams, and Truman Capote.[7] While it is true that all of these writers have produced similarly Gothic stories, their purposes for using this device are not the same.

Truman Capote's *Other Voices, Other Rooms* is a touchstone of the new American Gothic; it is a sustained terrifying story including many features characteristic of the genre. The passage from which the title derives is a description and historical account of the Cloud Hotel—a decaying ruin by the time Joel Knox, the central character, sees it. The legend explaining its demise includes a "drowning pond," from which ghostly arms appear to pull victims under, and a suicide by fire, occasioned by the insoluble mystery of the haunted pond. The vigorous family that owned the hotel in its days of magnificence has degenerated into the grotesque people who surround and terrify Joel: Cousin Randolph, Mr. Sansom, and Amy, each grotesque in a different way. The isolation of these charac-

7. "Flannery O'Connor's *Wise Blood,*" *Critique,* II (Fall 1958), 3.

ters is particularly significant; they live in the midst of
decay and degeneration, entirely apart from the larger
world. The Gothic properties of the story serve to enhance the central image of decay, suggesting on the
allegorical level that Joel Knox, the protagonist who
has lost his mother and searches for his father, seeks
meaning and identity in a world so broken that the
choices it offers are between several kinds of horror and
defeat. Although victory and the realization of a
healthy world of sound values are impossible in the
wasteland of *Other Voices, Other Rooms,* there is the
knowledge that something better once existed and the
romantic dream that it can be found again. Joel Knox
does not find that better world, but in some of the short
stories, it is found, only to be ironically lost again or
proven illusory in the first place. Whether or not Capote's stories are sustained Gothic ones, they often use
grotesque features, not gratuitously but thematically—
to image forth a world of decay, chaos, and psychological horror.

Carson McCullers's world view, like Capote's, finds
natural expression in shocking and terrifying images of
distortion and Gothic terror. Both writers employ outward horrors to reflect internal, psychological ones and
to characterize a nightmarish world which necessitates
and yet prevents the protagonists from adjusting to it or
changing it. In her stories there is a constant and pathetic wish on the part of her best characters for something better—for the recapturing of former happiness,
the fulfillment of love, or the chance to have a complete
and fruitful relationship with someone. Grotesqueness
is used to convey the condition of the world and its

effect on the characters; physical deformities sometimes appear, and perverse relationships are common: in *Reflections in a Golden Eye,* for example, one finds adultery, voyeurism, homosexuality, self-mutilation, suicide, and murder. This short novel is concerned thematically with the mystery of personal mismatches and the complementary reflection of the self in others. The characters do not arrive at any insight into themselves; they are driven by grotesque psychological forces. There is no epiphany, as there is no adjustment. The novel seems sympathetic with the torment; yet it is not a novel of social message asking tolerance for misfits, nor is it about sin. It simply presents the complex horror of life. As Oliver Evans points out, all of McCullers's novels end in frustration, the collapse of one dream of escape being followed by other dreams equally futile.[8] Grotesqueness is the product of living in such a world.

Both Capote and McCullers employ Gothic modes in order to explore internal reactions to external conditions, and to this extent they are concerned with the soul. Their representations are so highly objective, however, that one feels strongly the absence of a broader frame of reference which would enable him to make value judgments of the events. Irving Malin's study, *New American Gothic,* demonstrates that such fiction depends heavily on psychological matters—particularly narcissism—but when he attempts to interpret Flannery O'Connor's fiction by the same standards, it is obvious that he has misunderstood her use of the grotesque in

8. "Spiritual Isolation in Carson McCullers," *South: Modern Southern Literature in its Cultural Setting,* edited by Louis D. Rubin, Jr., and Robert D. Jacobs, p. 340.

the belief that outward similarity entails thematic one-ness. Capote and McCullers attempt to convey the horror of isolation, solipsism, and the buried life: Flannery O'Connor conveys the horror of responsibility, judgment, and the burden of morality, all presupposing a set of values that transcend the individual and dignify him by their demands. The deformities and aberrations of her characters and situations often call attention to horrors similar to those found in Capote's and McCullers's fiction, but one is aware that these horrors exist within the context of a significant ideal which is mysterious, but actual and realizable.

Because Flannery O'Connor uses Gothic modes to express the positive responsibilities and the quality of dignity of which man is capable, she must be considered as one of a different tradition of Gothic writers, the most important of whom is William Faulkner. The meaning of his Stockholm address is an excellent explanation of what interests these exploiters of the grotesque: When he speaks of the long sustained physical fear that we can now even bear, his point is that the condition has led writers to ignore the problems of the spirit and the human heart in favor of those of the glands. Faulkner would have them concerned with honor, pride, and hope, compassion, pity, and sacrifice. In *As I Lay Dying* (a novel which Flannery O'Connor urged Robert Fitzgerald to read and which he says was "close to her heart as a writer"[9]) is perhaps the best example of Faulkner's use of the grotesque to present matters of the spirit. In this novel grotesqueness is more

9. Robert Fitzgerald, "Introduction," *Everything That Rises Must Converge,* by Flannery O'Connor, p. xv.

evident than in Capote or McCullers: Vardaman's conception of his mother as a fish and his boring holes in her coffin; Dewey Dell's unwed pregnancy and her later seduction in the drug store where she goes to buy pills to bring on an abortion; Cash's broken leg encased in cement; Addie's rotting corpse; Darl's attempt to destroy the coffin by burning down a barn; and the choice of Anse, Addie's husband, on a new wife before Addie is in the ground. To list the grotesque details is to call up some of the most significant images in the book; they differ from those found in Capote and McCullers in the depths of meaning which they objectify. Faulkner is interested in and develops some of the same psychological realism as that found in the other writers, but he also invests the psychology with meanings that transcend it. Thus he brings the reader to consider the enduring qualities that define man at his worst and at his best. Reading Faulkner's grotesque stories, one has the feeling that even though the world is filled with depravity, decay, and frustration, there is nevertheless something more important, an intangible and often mysterious exponent of all such features, which redeem them.

At least two other prominent Southern writers who often write in the Gothic mode, Robert Penn Warren and Eudora Welty, achieve a realization of the depth and positiveness that are found in Faulkner. The themes that arise from their use of the Gothic mode are essentially spiritual ones, for they speak of matters of the soul and not matters of the glands or the nervous system. Flannery O'Connor, too, uses the grotesque for this same purpose, but unlike any of the other writers

mentioned, her concern is specifically Christian, as she
herself has explained:

My own feeling is that writers who see by the light of their
Christian faith will have, in these times, the sharpest eyes
for the grotesque, for the perverse, and for the unaccepta-
ble. . . . The novelist with Christian concerns will find in
modern life distortions which are repugnant to him, and his
problem will be to make these appear as distortions to an
audience which is used to seeing them as natural; and he
may well be forced to take ever more violent means to get
his vision across to this hostile audience.[10]

This quotation makes clear the fact that Miss
O'Connor's use of the Gothic and the grotesque, so far
as she understands her own work, does not place her in
"The Paul Bowles–Flannery O'Connor cult of the Gratuitous Grotesque."[11] Nearly all serious critics of Flannery O'Connor's work have corrected this misconcep-
tion. William Peden, for example, says that she is "not
a journalist or a scavenger fumbling with Gothic horrors
and monstrosities for their own sakes."[12] Although she
admits that it is the nature of her talent to give life to
grotesque characters such as the Misfit and the Bible
salesman, Manley Pointer,[13] she has borne out the critics'
principal defense of her predilection by observing that
the value of an apparently vile life is indicated by God's
dying to save it, as the chapters dealing with the re-

10. "The Fiction Writer and His Country," pp. 162–163.
11. William Esty, "In America, Intellectual Bomb Shelters,"
Commonweal, March 7, 1958, p. 588.
12. *The American Short Story*, p. 129.
13. Letter to James F. Farnham, quoted in his article, "The
Grotesque in Flannery O'Connor," *America*, May 13, 1961, p.
277.

ligious themes of her work show. She feels that the corruptions of life must be made believable if salvation is to have meaning to an audience which is spiritually numb.[14] She justifies her grotesque method to express a religious subject when she observes that "to the hard of hearing you shout, and for the almost blind you draw large and startling figures."[15]

Even though grotesqueness is a prevailing, but not gratuitous, characteristic of Flannery O'Connor's fiction, its incidence and its purpose vary within the stories. In some of the stories, grotesqueness is so frequent and the horror of it so heavy that they could be classified as Gothic. Throughout all of the stories and novels, whether or not truly Gothic, one finds tendencies toward the Gothic mode in the functions of the grotesque: grotesque motifs of displacement and identity; grotesque imagery involving deformity and feeblemindedness, illness and disease, animals and machines; the grotesque landscape of distorted natural imagery; and the literal grotesque of the everyday world.

"A Good Man Is Hard to Find" is an obvious example of a Gothic story. Its outstanding horror is the concluding mass murder of the vacationing family, and this rather slow-paced event represents roughly half of the story. The imminence of this horror is felt throughout the narrative, however; the Misfit's presence in the gen-

14. Flannery O'Connor, "The Church and the Fiction Writer," *America*, March 30, 1957, p. 733.
15. O'Connor, "The Fiction Writer and His Country," p. 163.

eral area through which the family will travel on their
trip from Atlanta to Florida foreshadows the meeting
between him and the family. In the opening paragraph
the grandmother warns them of the danger as she reads
the newspaper account of the criminal's escape from the
penitentiary. Later when they stop at the Tower for
lunch, the grandmother and the waitress again mention
the Misfit, and the aphorism which gives the story its
grimly ironic title.

In addition to foreshadowings about the Misfit,
the first half of the story contains Gothic qualities independent of the final murder except as they portray spiritual insensitivity which seems bound for violent correction. The automobile trip is a study in the pathos of
common vulgarity and quiet desperation in an almost
infernal domestic situation. The mother is lumpish: she
has "a face as broad and innocent as a cabbage" and a
green kerchief tied around her head with two points
"like rabbit's ears" (p. 9) ; she had little to say about
anything and goes to sleep in the car. The children,
June Star and John Wesley, are ill-mannered and brat-
tish; they read comic magazines, disrespectfully dispar-
age the grandmother's home state of Tennessee as "a
hillbilly dumping ground" (p. 11), callously sneer at
the "broken-down place" where they eat lunch, and
take delight in the automobile accident. They join
forces with the grandmother in torturing their father:
she insists that they leave the main road to visit a plantation which she remembers from childhood; John Wesley viciously kicks his father in the kidneys and screams
until Bailey Boy reluctantly acquiesces: "this is the only
time we're going to stop for anything like this. This is

the one and only time" (p. 17). His words ominously and ironically suggest the fatality of their decision; their strong sense of inevitability enhances the Gothic quality.

The countryside itself becomes an aspect of horror in the first half of the story, its grotesque details overshadowing the real beauty which the grandmother sometimes perceives, as when she notices with pleasure details of scenery such as simple outcroppings of blue granite, "brilliant red clay banks slightly streaked with purple," and trees "full of silver-white sunlight" (p. 11). By contrast, the family ignores such beauty, noticing instead features such as a graveyard, a half-naked Negro child standing in the doorway of a shack, and the series of garish signs that lead them to "a part stucco and part wood filling station and dance hall" presided over by "a fat man named Red Sammy Butts" (p. 13), who appears initially with his head under a truck while a chained gray monkey chatters above him. Inside the "long dark room" the mother plays "The Tennessee Waltz" and a fast number on the nickelodeon, providing the opportunity for the grandmother's grotesque suggestion that Bailey dance with her, and then the opportunity for a ludicrous tap dance by June Star.

The dirt road to the plantation house (which is, as the grandmother belatedly realizes, in Tennessee, not Georgia) becomes a significant feature of the Gothic tissue. Near Toombsboro, Georgia, the road yields swirls of "pink dust," abounds in sharp curves, dangerous embankments, and deep red clay gulleys. The car overturns when the cat, Pitty Sing, frightened by the grandmother's sudden motion when she realizes her error, springs onto Bailey's shoulder; the mother and baby are thrown out and the others dashed to the floor of the car. The accident is dully assimilated by all except June Star and John Wesley, who are disappointed that nobody was killed.

The Misfit, Hiram, and Bobby Lee arrive in "a big black battered hearse-like automobile" (p. 20), its unnaturally slow movement signaling the terrifyingly methodical, patient performance of the mass murder. The Misfit's evil nature is emphasized by contrast with his bespectacled, scholarly appearance and his childlike mannerisms; as the grandmother desperately appeals for her life to him as a good man, he uses the butt of his gun to draw a circle on the ground and remains preoccupied with his doodling and his family background while Bailey, John Wesley, the mother, the baby, and June Star are taken to the woods and shot. A particularly chilling detail is the casualness with which Bobby Lee returns from the shooting of Bailey and drags the murdered man's "yellow shirt with bright blue parrots on it" (p. 26). The Misfit puts on the shirt with hardly a pause in his running conversation with Bailey's mother. The impact of this action is implicit and not garishly described; its significance lies in the symbolic identity established between Bailey and the Misfit, whom the grandmother later calls one of her own children. Such grotesque inversions in which a distinctly dissimilar character replaces a child, parent, or close relative are frequent in Flannery O'Connor's fiction and constitute one element of the Gothic quality. Similar instances appear in "Everything That Rises Must Converge" when Julian's mother and the Negro woman swap children on the bus; in "The Partridge Festival" when Calhoun recognizes the lunatic murderer Singleton as his kinsman; in "Greenleaf" when Mrs. May feels that the Greenleaf twins are more her children in spirit than Wesley and Scofield. In "A Good Man Is Hard to Find" the grandmother's recognition of the Misfit as her child is her moment of saving charity, and its consequence is the sudden and violent end to the Misfit's patience and stern gentleness as he shoots her three times and settles back matter-of-factly to clean his glasses. The sustained horror of this story remains unrelieved in the last line, when the Misfit denies life in his declaration, "It's no real pleasure in life" (*Good Man,* p. 29).

"The Lame Shall Enter First" may also be considered Gothic, for it is pervaded with terror and concerns three major characters, all grotesque. Sheppard, in his secular, sociological attempt to love his neighbor as himself, represents the contemporary distortion of one of the basic truths of Christianity; Norton, his son, has been traumatized by the death of his mother and the insensitivity of his father, and Rufus Johnson is a depraved clubfoot. Rufus's grotesqueness is represented by his foot; it is reiterated in other incidents, the implicit significance of which, like the clubfoot, connects them with the religious theme of the story. In one instance Rufus comes to Sheppard's home, finds Norton alone, and desecrates Norton's memory of his mother by scattering some of her clothes and adorning himself with others in a grotesque dance, singing, "Gonter rock, rattle and roll. Can't please that woman, to save my doggone soul" (*Everything,* p. 157). Later, when Sheppard

challenges his belief in Jesus, Rufus claims to prove it
by eating the pages from a Bible which he has stolen.

Norton's ugliness is less physical than it is a matter of
action, largely traceable to his father's rejection of him.
He is first seen eating a disgusting breakfast of cake
covered with ketchup and peanut butter while his
father, ironically preoccupied with explaining the pitiful sight of Rufus Johnson eating from a garbage can,
looks on without objection. Sheppard lectures his child
for his selfishness, enumerating Norton's many advan-
tages and asking for charity toward the Rufus Johnsons
of the world. When he mentions the child's mother, he
tells the boy not to grieve over losing her, but to be
grateful that his mother is not in the state penitentiary.
This insensitivity to the boy's grief for his mother causes
an outburst of weeping. Sheppard construes this grief as
selfishness and is dull to the meaning of his own observation that the child was not selfish when his mother was
alive. He continues to berate his son, and when he
suggests Rufus's need for a new shoe, Norton vomits
and waits "with his mouth open over the plate as if he
expected his heart to come up next" (p. 148).

This sequence is not made revolting to shock the
reader gratuitously; its severity exists because Flannery
O'Connor realizes that her audience, like Sheppard, is
largely blind, especially when dramatic social righteousness is in conflict with uncomplicated private devotion.
She has said that she cannot write about anything subtle, and this means that she draws issues clearly and
allows no mistake regarding moral problems which are
poorly defined by our society. Norton's significance is
thus established quite early in the story and is restated

frequently in other grotesque scenes. One of these depicts an alone, isolated, tortured Norton in a dark room illuminated occasionally by lightning and eerily invaded by the villain:

> That afternoon Norton was alone in the house, squatting on the floor of his room arranging packages of flower seeds in rows around himself. Rain slashed against the window panes and rattled in the gutters. The room had grown dark but every few minutes it was lit by silent lightning and the seed packages showed up gaily on the floor. He squatted motionless like a large pale frog in the midst of this potential garden. All at once his eyes became alert. Without warning the rain had stopped. The silence was heavy as if the downpour had been hushed by violence. He remained motionless, only his eyes turning.
>
> Into the silence came the distinct click of a key turning in the front door lock. The sound was a very deliberate one. It drew attention to itself and held it as if it were controlled more by a mind than by a hand. The child leapt up and got into the closet (pp. 152–153).

When he feels it is safe again, Norton leaves the closet and is suddenly confronted by Rufus, limping, dripping wet, bony-faced, and dressed in black: "His look went through the child like a pin and paralyzed him" (p. 153).

Such a scene is very close to the effect and the detail of traditional Gothic fiction; the darkness, the storm, the isolation, the villain, and the terror of the innocent victim are all included. The irresponsibility of the victim's parent allows him to become completely subject to the villain from this point on, just as the traditional Gothic victim is often absolutely helpless. Norton goes off "like a mechanical toy" when Rufus orders a sandwich and milk from him, showing the effect of the pin and paralysis metaphor used earlier. In subsequent action, Norton flees to the villain-hero as a substitute for his father: he accepts Rufus's explanations rather than his father's, much as Bishop becomes subject to Tarwater in *The Violent Bear It Away*.

Like Tarwater, Rufus, though evil in one sense, provides the boy with a credo sounder than he has formerly had, insofar as it solves the problem of his grief for his lost mother and his lack of love from his father. Just as Bishop is both saved and destroyed by Tarwater, Norton's palliative discoveries are attended by the violent recourse of suicide. In the novel and the story, the heroes are thus similar to those of traditional Gothic fiction, whose motive is essentially moral but manifests itself in corruption and violence because of its excess and because of the grotesqueness of the character himself. In American literature, Hawthorne's Chillingworth, Melville's Pierre, and Faulkner's Sutpen are characters of this type.

The sustained horror of this story emerges from the combination of effects prompted by the villain-hero Rufus Johnson, by the innocent victim Norton, and by the grim spectacle of a father's failure to know when love is needed and his inability to recognize moral depravity. The Gothic effect is not relieved, but enhanced, by the epiphany of Sheppard, for it is followed by his tragic and ugly discovery that knowledge has come to him too late to save Norton. This scene is the capstone of the thoroughly Gothic structure:

[Sheppard] groaned with joy. He would make everything up to him. He would never let him suffer again. He would be mother and father. He jumped up and ran to his room, to kiss him, to tell him that he loved him, that he would never fail him again.

The light was on in Norton's room but the bed was empty. He turned and dashed up the attic stairs and at the top reeled back like a man on the edge of a pit. The tripod had fallen and the telescope lay on the floor. A few feet over it, the child hung in the jungle of shadows, just below the beam from which he had launched his flight into space (p. 190).

Although both of them are positive stories thematically in that they are Christian, "A Good Man Is Hard to Find" and "The Lame Shall Enter First" both end in violent tragedy. The other two Gothic stories are not severe in their conclusions. "The Artificial Nigger" ends happily in the reconciliation of Nelson and Mr. Head; "Judgement Day" portrays a violent death, but Tanner is ready to die, and the conclusion emphasizes the joyful entry into the hereafter to such an extent that the grotesqueness of the old man's death is subordinated. Both of these stories are Gothic in terms of their depiction of a real world which is, in the eyes of the participants, a strange, hostile, frightening environment. The general effect is surrealistic.

The dominant motif of "Judgement Day" is that of the displacement of Tanner, and this is a mode of the grotesque which is found in a number of stories. "The Displaced Person" is, of course, a key story in establishing the idea, but its presence throughout the work of Flannery O'Connor is noticed by several critics, among them Caroline Gordon, who says that all of O'Connor's characters may be considered displaced persons.[16] Miss Gordon is referring to theological displacement in that the characters are so often living outside the state of grace. Certainly this is the correct meaning, and it is this meaning that gives the thematic justification for the grotesqueness entailed in the representation of characters who are not only theologically displaced, but displaced in physical and sometimes psychological ways too.

Mr. Guizac, for example, in "The Displaced Person," is essentially an object rather than a person in the eyes of the usual residents of Mrs. McIntyre's farm. His foreign language and mannerisms dissociate him from them, thus he is grotesque when seen through their eyes. Mrs. Shortley thinks of the entire Guizac family as an aggregation resembling the three bears with wooden shoes, and Mr. Shortley identifies Mr. Guizac with an anonymous German soldier who threw a hand grenade at him during the First World War. Other grotesque details attributable to Mrs. Shortley's distorted view are numerous. Sledgewig Guizac's name sounds to her as if it should apply to a bug, "as if you named a boy Boll-weevil" (*Good Man*, p. 199) , and she sees Mr. Guizac as a monkey jumping on the tractor and Mrs. Guizac as "shaped like a peanut" (p. 198) . The most startling image used to convey the outsider's mental distortion is the recurrent one of a Nazi concentration camp:

Mrs. Shortley recalled a newsreel she had seen once of a small room piled high with bodies of dead naked people all in a heap, their arms and legs tangled together, a head thrust in here, a head there, a foot, a knee, a part that

16. *Op. cit.*, p. 9.

should have been covered up sticking out, a hand raised clutching nothing. . . . Mrs. Shortley had the sudden intuition that the Gobblehooks, like rats with typhoid fleas, could have carried all those murderous ways over the water with them directly to this place (p. 200).

Only after Mr. Guizac's offer of his cousin to the Negro Sulk offends Mrs. McIntyre, does her vision begin to yield grotesque glimpses of the displaced person, as Mrs. Shortley's had from the very first. Although she submits to his courtliness and foreign ways as long as he is innocent in her eyes, she later sees him "as if she were watching him through a gunsight" and views him in the distance as "no larger than a grasshopper" (p. 236). These grotesque images accompany her decision to get rid of Mr. Guizac because "He doesn't fit in. I have to have somebody who fits in" (p. 237). The crucial point of the displacement motif in this story is that the figure who is grotesque because he does not fit in is only apparently so, while those who thus apprehend him are the truly grotesque. As Robert Drake expresses it, "Surely, Miss O'Connor would have agreed with Pope that all seems infected that the infected spy."[17] That Mr. and Mrs. Shortley and Mrs. McIntyre may be understood as the actual displaced people, Flannery O'Connor gives them grotesque characteristics, the important difference being that their grotesqueness is apparent from the author's objective point of view rather than from the limited, subjective point of view of an infected vision; Mr. Guizac is nearly always seen indirectly, while the others are largely described directly by the author. Mrs. Shortley is described directly at the

17. *Flannery O'Connor: A Critical Essay*, p. 40.

moment of death; significantly she is in the automobile as the Shortleys are moving, being displaced from the farm. Her grotesque death is presented in the very images which she had associated with Mr. Guizac, those of the concentration camp. The same absence of a qualifying point of view is found at the conclusion of the story when Mrs. McIntyre falls ill and is forced to be displaced from her farm; the grotesqueness is physical, but her displacement is theological:

A numbness developed in one of her legs and her hands and head began to jiggle and eventually she had to stay in bed all the time with only a colored woman to wait on her. Her eyesight grew steadily worse and she lost her voice altogether (*Good Man,* p. 251).

Further examples of how displacement generates grotesqueness appear throughout the stories and novels. Asbury in "The Enduring Chill" is objectively grotesque and his vision is distorted because neither New York nor Timberboro is his true element. The boys in "A Circle in the Fire" are grotesque in the city because they despise it and equally grotesque on Mrs. Cope's farm because they do not truly belong there either. Hulga Hopewell in "Good Country People" is not only grotesque physically, but grotesque in the displacement resulting from the disparity between her education and that of the people who surround her. And Mrs. May, competent and practical, has become grotesquely rigid in her efficiency partly because of her determination to conquer the demands of the alien and new world of the farm left to her when her husband died.

A second major grotesque motif is that of identity, not in the character's simply discovering who he is, but in the sometimes-surrealistic blending or converging of two or more characters, such as that found in "Judgement Day." In New York, old Tanner is entirely unable to grasp the essential difference between the Negro actor who lives across the hall from his daughter and the Negroes he has known in the South. Whereas he had been a confident and mature person in that other environment, in New York his every action goes awry, from his attempt to befriend the Negro to his foolish and fatal attempt to return to Corinth, Georgia. Because he feels alien and confined, Tanner's mind reaches back in time and place in an attempt to escape the identity thrust upon him. His efforts to reaffirm his former self lead him to confront the convergence of his own identity with Coleman Parrum and even with the Negro doctor Foley, who had gained a kind of sovereignty over Tanner in much the same fashion that Tanner had won the upper hand with Coleman.

Reflection is often part of the imagery used to convey the merging of personalities. Examples appear in "Everything That Rises Must Converge," "A Good Man Is Hard to Find," "The Partridge Festival," and "Greenleaf." Reflection imagery occurs too in the strong resemblance of Mr. Head and Nelson in "The Artificial Nigger." Mark Fortune in "A View of the Woods" is ironically delighted at the likeness of himself apparent in his granddaughter, Mary Fortune Pitts. In *Wise Blood* Hazel Motes is grotesquely reflected in every detail by the false prophet Solace Layfield, and the entire story of Enoch Emery is interspersed with images suggesting that his double is by turns the animals at the zoo, the shrunken mummy, and Gonga, the gorilla suit. *The*

Violent Bear It Away depends heavily on the motif of identity; the resemblances between Mason Tarwater, Francis Marion Tarwater, George Rayber, and Bishop are frequently drawn, and the accompanying grotesqueness in nearly every instance carries a sense of the mysterious and a thematic point related to Tarwater's struggle to identify himself with or against his great-uncle or Rayber; the resulting complexity of Tarwater's nature can be seen in this passage:

With Tarwater's eyes on him, [Rayber] felt subjected to a pressure that killed his energy before he had a chance to exert it. The eyes were the eyes of the crazy student father, the personality was the old man's, and somewhere between the two, Rayber's own image was struggling to survive and he was not able to reach it *(Violent, p. 115)*.

Inherited characteristics weigh so heavily upon Rayber that he considers himself maimed by his resistance to them:

The affliction was in the family. It lay hidden in the line of blood that touched them, flowing from some ancient source, some desert prophet or polesitter, until, its power unabated, it appeared in the old man, and him and, he surmised, in the boy. Those it touched were condemned to fight it constantly or be ruled by it. The old man had been ruled by it. He, at the cost of a full life, staved it off. What the boy would do hung in the balance (p. 114).

An interest in blood inheritance and its meaning to those who seek their proper identity is quite common in Gothic novels, but in *The Violent Bear It Away,* in some of the short stories, and particularly in *Wise Blood,* the ideas relevant to the motif are religious. The loss of self and the irrevocability of blood are terrifying only so long as their meanings exist apart from the numinous.

Although Flannery O'Connor has written stories which are thoroughly Gothic and there are several grotesque motifs found throughout her work, the presence of the grotesque is not limited by these categories. Grotesqueness is so pervasive in the stories and novels that it may be considered as part of the texture of her fiction.

As the content of the Gothic stories demonstrates, grotesqueness is often used to indicate the moral and spiritual conditions of the characters. Several classifications of such images may be found: (1) deformity and feeblemindedness, (2) illness and disease, (3) animal imagery, and (4) machine imagery. Deformed characters are relatively few, and their general meaning fairly consistent: their conditions reflect spiritual incompleteness or lameness. Mr. Shiftlet in "The Life You Save May Be Your Own" has only one arm, Hulga Hopewell in "Good Country People" wears an artificial leg, and Rufus Johnson in "The Lame Shall Enter First" has a clubfoot; each is in some way a moral derelict. An excellent example of this meaning of deformity is given in an image of dismemberment in *The Violent Bear It Away;* Mason Tarwater is telling his great-nephew that the boy's mother was a whore:

He knew what they were and to what they were liable to come, and just as Jezebel was discovered by dogs, an arm here and a foot there, so said his great-uncle, it had almost been with his own mother and grandmother. The two of them, along with his grandfather, had been killed in an automobile crash, leaving only the schoolteacher alive in that family (*Violent,* p. 40) .

On the other hand, deformity may exist to demonstrate that man's condition is normally corrupt and that he is better off in accepting it, as the hermaphrodite does in "A Temple of the Holy Ghost," and as the one-armed good Samaritan implicitly does in *Wise Blood* when he helps Haze Motes to start his broken-down car and refuses any payment from Haze, who is apparently physically sound. Feeble-mindedness is most often associated with innocence, as Bishop in *The Violent Bear It Away* and Lucynell Crater in "The Life You Save May Be Your Own" indicate.

The imagery of illness and disease is never ambiguous, but it might convey different and opposite meanings from one story to another. That cancer on Mr. Paradise's ear in "The River" cannot be healed signifies his internal lack of health; this is reiterated in his mockery of the healing at the river and of religion in general. Mrs. Connin's husband, in the same story, suffers from stomach ulcers and, in spite of her advice, will not thank Jesus or anyone else for the portion of his stomach remaining after surgery. In "A Circle in the Fire" the ignorant and narrow Mrs. Pritchard is thankful that she has nothing more wrong with her than four abscessed teeth, but the reader is aware of a deeper abscess. Even extreme age is a form of illness of the body as well as the soul in "A Late Encounter with the Enemy"; General Sash's most startling line and his most convincing indication of life is his vilification of everything: "God damn every goddam thing to hell" (*Good*

Man, p. 163). In "A Stroke of Good Fortune," Ruby Hill considers pregnancy not as a sacred responsibility to bring forth new life, but as an illness to which even heart trouble would be preferable; at other times she deludes herself that her pains are from gas. Conversely, the grotesque stories told by Mrs. Pritchard in "A Circle in the Fire" about a woman who gave birth while in an iron lung are startling images illustrating the remarkable endurance of one woman determined to fulfill her feminine role in spite of the most formidable obstacle. A similar juxtaposition within the narrative of "Good Country People" gives meaning to Mrs. Freeman's revolting chatter about her daughter Carramae's morning sickness in terms of Hulga Hopewell's sterility and her cynical intention to use sex as a weapon by seducing the representative of good country people, the Bible salesman. Asbury Fox's undulant fever in "The Enduring Chill" and Mrs. McIntyre's nervous disorder in "The Displaced Person" signify their poor spiritual health. Mrs. Greenleaf claims to have used prayer healing to rid one man of worms when "half his gut was eat out" (*Everything,* p. 51), and Tarwater believes that the nagging of his religious dedication is worms. The self-inflicted blindness of Hazel Motes is the sign of his submission to God.

Animal imagery describing people traditionally carries pejorative meaning. This is the usual effect of the many comparisons between characters and animals in Flannery O'Connor's work, although in some instances the reader is expected simply to see detail more clearly. The Biblical uncleanliness of swine is perhaps the key to the frequent use of comparisons involving them. Mr.

Paradise and the mischievous Connin children are compared to pigs, and Mary Grace calls Mrs. Turpin a wart
hog; in *The Violent Bear It Away,* Tarwater says that
Bishop will rot like a hog. Although the complexity of
these images varies from story to story, all of them point
to the essentially fallen and corrupt, sometimes the
unrelievedly unclean, nature of man. The same point
pervades the many descriptions of Enoch Emery in
Wise Blood; at one point he is seen crouching in the
shrubbery like an animal on all fours and in another
instance he walks "down the street as if he were led by a
silent melody or by one of those whistles that only dogs
hear."[18] Enoch envies the animals at the zoo; he sometimes imagines what it would feel like to be one of them
and achieves his own grotesque triumph when he im-
brutes himself in the gorilla outfit of Gonga. Other
examples of animal imagery arise, not from the corrupt
nature of the characters so described, but from the corruption of the vision of the one who apprehends them
in grotesque fashion. Mark Fortune sees his daughter's
entire family as a chorus of frogs around the dinner
table. Ruby Hill is revolted by Mr. Jerger, the old man
who lives in the apartment building; to her, he looks
like a goat, and his odor is "like putting her nose under
a buzzard's wing" (*Good Man,* p. 77). Actually, neither
Mr. Jerger nor the Pittses are so animal-like as the ones
who describe them.

Characters associated with machines usually have severely limited human responses and function mechani-

18. Flannery O'Connor, *Wise Blood,* p. 153. Further quotations
from this work will be identified with the abbreviation *WB* and
a page number in parentheses.

cally rather than humanly. In *Wise Blood,* this deficiency is made broadly applicable to society in general
through the juxtaposition of a man who hawks potato
peelers and Asa Hawks, who merchandises Christian
salvation. Hazel Motes tries to believe that his automobile is sufficient to save him, and the degenerate Sabbath Lily Hawks turns her head "as if it worked on a
screw" (*WB,* p. 103). Enoch Emery's heart is said to
beat with a sound like a motorcycle racing around an
enclosed sphere at the county fair, and in *The Violent
Bear It Away* Rayber's heart is often compared to a
machine. Tarwater is fascinated by Rayber's hearing
aid, and his questions about it clearly indicate the significance of his uncle's deficiency and the reason for the
necessity of a machine to bolster his unsound human
responses: "What you wired for? . . . Does your head
light up?" (*Violent,* p. 103). When Bishop is drowned,
the machine causes a grotesque intensification of the
child's screams, which seem to come from inside Rayber
rather than from the lake, and his own guilt in the
murderous aspect of Tarwater's act is indicated in this
manner. Because machinery has practically nothing to
do with the necessities for salvation, Tarwater has not
been instructed in this area by his great-uncle; he is
ignorant as to the use of the telephone when he has to
reach his uncle, and he scoffs at Rayber's awe at the
miracle of the airplane by commenting that buzzards
can fly.

Another broad area of the grotesque is inherent in
Tarwater's remark about the buzzards; his comment
suggests that he places more faith in what is natural
than in what is man-made. His attitude is typical of

Flannery O'Connor's use of nature as a backdrop for
her action, sometimes neutrally, but more often to contrast the image of eternity and permanence with the
flux and violence of the world of men. Images involving
the woods and the sun are most frequently used for this
purpose. An outstanding instance in which the woods
become a metaphysical landscape occurs in Hazel
Motes's impression of Jesus moving in his mind from
tree to tree. Several violent actions which ultimately
bring religious epiphany are set against such a background; in "A Good Man Is Hard to Find," the woods
are cited several times as the site of the murders of the
family: "Behind them the line of woods gaped like a
dark open mouth" (*Good Man*, p. 21). In "Greenleaf"
the violent action ending the story takes place in "a
green arena, encircled almost entirely by woods" (*Everything*, p. 50), and the emphasis on greenness is indicated in the name of the main character, Mrs. May, and
the entire working out of the action:

The morning was dry and clear. She drove through the
woods for a quarter of a mile and then out into the open
where there were fields on either side of the narrow road.
The exhilaration of carrying her point had sharpened her
senses. Birds were screaming everywhere, the grass was almost too bright to look at, the sky was an even piercing
blue. "Spring is here!" she said gaily (p. 48).

In "A View of the Woods," the pine trees mutely wit-
ness the terrifying scene in which Mark Fortune and his
granddaughter kill each other.

The image of the woods is sometimes merged with
that of the sun, as it is in *The Violent Bear It Away*,
when Mason Tarwater tells his great-nephew, "And

when I'm gone, you'll be better off in these woods by yourself with just as much light as the sun wants to let in than you'll be in the city with [Rayber]" (*Violent,* p. 24). The woods are a place of retreat from the secular world of Rayber, and the sun represents, as it traditionally does, the light of God, to be accepted but not forced. In "The River," the spiritually deprived Harry Ashfield wants "to dash off and snatch the sun which was rolling away ahead of them." (*Good Man,* p. 39). Later he sees "pieces of the white sun scattered in the river" (p. 44), to which he ultimately commits himself in the hope of achieving the kingdom of Christ. The sun in "A Circle in the Fire" seems to burn, as if to purge Mrs. Cope of her inordinate fear of fire, the symbol of her pride. In "Greenleaf" the sun is sometimes associated with the bull which brings death and epiphany to Mrs. May; in one instance it is described as being like a bullet. If one takes this image as a religious one, it has some similarity to such startling imagery as one finds in the metaphysical poets—for example, John Donne's sonnet in which God is compared to a battering ram at the door of a besieged city gate.

A grotesque landscape may also be the result of the deformed or transformed vision of a participant in the action. Thus celestial bodies are sometimes demeaned by proud characters who are not willing to show the humility of Mason Tarwater in accepting only so much light as the sun might give through the trees. Mrs. May, in "Greenleaf," at one time sees the sun setting as if it were descending a ladder, and to Mrs. Crater in "The Life You Save May Be Your Own," "A fat yellow moon appeared in the branches of the fig tree as if it were going to roost there with the chickens" (*Good Man,* p. 57) . The satanic voice in *The Violent Bear It Away* speaks to Tarwater of the dwarf sun; Hulga in "Good Country People" sees only a hazy landscape when her glasses are stolen by the Bible salesman; and Mr. Shiftlet, in "The Life You Save May Be Your Own," after deserting Lucynell, notices a turnip-shaped cloud. In *The Violent Bear It Away,* nature appears as a nightmare to Tarwater when he is drunk and derelict in his duty to bury his great uncle:

Some night bird complaining close by woke him up. It was not a screeching noise, only an intermittent hump-hump as if the bird had to recall his grievance each time before he repeated it. Clouds were moving convulsively across a black sky and there was a pink unsteady moon that appeared to be jerked up a foot or so and then dropped and jerked up again. This was because, as he observed in an instant, the sky was lowering, coming down fast to smother him. The bird screeched and flew off in time and Tarwater lurched into the middle of the stream bed and crouched on his hands and knees. The moon was reflected like pale fire in the few spots of water in the sand. He sprang at the wall of honeysuckle and began to tear through it, confusing the sweet familiar odor with the weight coming down on him. When he stood up on the other side, the black ground swung slowly and threw him down again. A flare of pink lightning lit the woods and he saw the black shapes of trees pierce out of the ground all around him. The night bird began to hump again from a thicket where he had settled (*Violent,* pp. 48–49) .

On the other hand, Tarwater apprehends nature differently when he is sober and somewhat ashamed:

He did not look up at the sky but he was unpleasantly aware of the stars. They seemed to be holes in his skull through which some distant unmoving light was watching him. It was as if he were alone in the presence of an immense silent eye (p. 85).

In this instance the grotesque representation of the heavenly bodies carries a different meaning, not to show that Tarwater has been transformed, for he has not, but to indicate the inescapable presence of God in his life. Later when Tarwater fears the realization of his great uncle's imperatives, his agitation is expressed in terms of his manner of apprehending the heavens:

The sun, from being only a ball of glare, was becoming distinct like a large pearl, as if sun and moon had fused in a brilliant marriage. The boy's narrowed eyes made a black spot of it. When he was a child he had several times, experimentally, commanded the sun to stand still, and once for as long as he watched it—a few seconds—it had stood still, but when he turned his back, it had moved. Now he would have liked for it to get out of the sky altogether or to be veiled in a cloud. He turned his face enough to rid his vision of it and was aware again of the country which seemed to lie beyond the silence, or in it, stretching off into the distance around him (*Violent,* pp. 221–222).

Ultimately, at the end of the novel, when he submits to the religious mission for which he has been prepared, the landscape merges with his vision of his future and his commitment to the sustaining strength of the fishes and loaves.

If man's jaded point of view distorts nature, so does his physical presence desecrate the landscape, as the littered plot of land where Tilman does business in "A View of the Woods" reveals. In *The Violent Bear It Away,* T. Fawcett Meeks and Tarwater stop at a filling station on the outskirts of the city, "a gaping concrete mouth with two red gas pumps set in front of it and a small glass office toward the back" (p. 80) ; its grotesqueness is repeated in descriptions of the city throughout the stories and novels. In *Wise Blood* Hazel Motes looks upon a landscape scarred by the evidence of man's presence.

The highway was ragged with filling stations and trailer camps and roadhouses. After a while there were stretches where red gulleys dropped off on either side of the road and behind them there were patches of field buttoned together with 666 posts. The sky leaked over all of it and then it began to leak into the car. The head of a string of pigs appeared snout-up over the ditch and he had to screech to a stop and watch the rear of the last pig disappear shaking into the ditch on the other side. He started the car again and went on. He had the feeling that everything he saw was a broken-off piece of some giant blank thing that he had forgotten had happened to him. A black pick-up truck turned off a side road in front of him. On the back of it an iron bed and a chair and table were tied, and on top of them, a crate of barred-rock chickens (pp. 74–75) .

The desecrated landscape is one manifestation of Flannery O'Connor's preoccupation with the ugliness of reality. She speaks of this kind of grotesqueness in a letter to Sister Mary Alice: "If you have a detail that is just the traditional kind of prettiness, reject it, and look for one that is closer to the heart of the matter, that is a little more grotesque, but that gives us a better idea of the reality of the thing."[19] To the writer with a close, hard, objective vision, the world contains a great deal of unpleasant reality that need not be distorted to appear grotesque. When man is seen against the background of

19. Quoted by Sister Mary Alice, "My Mentor, Flannery O'Connor," *Saturday Review*, May 29, 1965, p. 24.

Christian idealism, his characteristics, actions, and features of his personally created environment reveal, sometimes revoltingly, his fallen state. In "A Circle in the Fire" for instance, the common insolence and vulgarity of one of the boys conveys such an effect:

The large boy was stretched out in the hammock with his wrists crossed under his head and the cigarette stub in the center of his mouth. He spit it out in an arc just as Mrs. Cope came around the corner of the house with a plate of crackers. She stopped instantly as if a snake had been slung in her path (*Good Man,* p. 138).

In "The Life You Save May Be Your Own," Mr. Shiftlet offers Mrs. Crater a piece of chewing gum: "she only raised her upper lip to indicate she had no teeth" (*Good Man,* p. 55). Neither of these actions is distorted; they are a part of the ordinary ugliness and vulgarity that attend life in this world. There is an equal absence of distortion in the picture of Sulk, whose tongue hangs out and describes small circles as he examines a photograph of Mr. Guizac's young cousin. Similar examples may be found throughout the stories and novels.

Even when grotesqueness is rendered with the help of comparisons, there is such aptness that one feels the grotesqueness is the result of actuality, not the vehicle of the metaphor. In *Wise Blood,* for example, there are three women who are "dressed like parrots," and a dining car steward who moves about "like a crow" (p. 15). Mrs. Flood has "race-horse legs" and "hair clustered like grapes on her brow" (p. 220).

In *The Violent Bear It Away* Rayber searches for a gift to placate Tarwater after discarding the boy's disreputable clothes:

He stopped for gas at a pink stucco filling station where pottery and whirligigs were sold. While the car was being filled, he got out and looked for something to take as a peace offering, for he wanted the encounter to be pleasant if possible. His eye roved over a shelf of false hands, imitation buck teeth, boxes of simulated dog dung to put on the rug, wooden plaques with cynical mottos burnt on them. Finally he saw a combination corkscrew-bottleopener that fit in the palm of the hand. He bought it and left (p. 188).

This is the ludicrous world as Flannery O'Connor sees it; her selection of detail is not the caricaturist's method of distortion, but she sees the actual horror and ugliness of the world. Its grotesqueness results from her technique of drawing large, of seeing reality as if examining nearby phenomena through a telescope or as if directing her readers' eyes through a microscope to show them what should be visible to the naked eye. Whether grotesqueness in her work is a part of the Gothic impulse, whether it is in the distorted vision of spiritually myopic characters, whether it is in the spectacle of grotesque behavior brought about by the characters' lack of knowledge of themselves and their true country, or whether grotesqueness is simply the everyday ugliness that exists as a testament to the disparity between this world and that of the ideal, Flannery O'Connor's purpose is always the same: to see actuality without undue sentimental or romantic regret that paradise is not of this world, and to demonstrate that, for all its horror, life here is merely passage by the dragon as one goes to the Father of Souls. This passage, she believes, is the concern of any story of depth and demands courage on the part of the reader. The storyteller too must have considerable courage to present the horror of the passage as he sees it.

Chapter 7 Comic
and
Grim
Laughter

THE South has pro-
duced a number of writers whose work is rich in humor,
from the Southwestern humorists to Faulkner, Caldwell, and Eudora Welty. This humor has often depended upon regional peculiarities of dialect and custom and has shown a high incidence of grim humor
arising from an essentially grotesque or revolting situation and calling forth a laughter that dwindles into
stricken astonishment that pathos and horror should be
funny. Flannery O'Connor's humor extends these traditions and provokes laughter that is sometimes purely
comic but often grim. In either case, it is good-humored
or corrective rather than brutal or mocking.

Flannery O'Connor's letters and the remarks about
her by friends reveal that she was delighted by humor
and had an abundant talent for it. As cartoonist for her
college newspaper, *Colonnade,* and as illustrator for the
yearbook, *Spectrum,* she demonstrated a sharp eye for
the ludicrous and incongruous. As a mature and suc-
cessful writer, her sense of humor found expression not
only in her stories, but in a predominantly humorous

article for *Holiday,* "Living With a Peacock," in which one can see significant features of the O'Connor technique: a bantam chicken that walks backwards and is photographed by Pathé News; peacocks that eat everything from Startena to Lady Bankshire roses; and a truckdriver who stops for a strutting peacock and says, "Get a load of that bastard."[1] As funny as the entire article is, it contains an undercurrent of serious and profound significance; the details of the peacock's appearance and habits, its rarity and yet its stamina and proliferation convey more than shallow local, personal, and humorous meaning to anyone who knows that the peacock is a traditional Christian symbol. The humor in her fiction is also set against a sober and sometimes tragic background. Robert Fitzgerald observes that "the presence of her humor is like the presence of grace."[2]

In "Living With a Peacock," the image of these magnificent birds eating the flowers at Andalusia Farm is humorous in itself, but Flannery O'Connor enhances the effect by naming the exact kinds of flowers, Lady Bankshire and Herbert Hoover roses. Such names are humorous because of incongruity—as proud as the names are, the browsing peacock might just as well be pecking to shreds a lowly zinnia, the blossom of a jimson weed, or even a common, unnamed variety of rose. The names of things and people have had from primitive times an aura of the mystery of being, a sacredness attached to the reverence man holds for creation at large. When the word is detached from its object, this

1. September 1961, p. 111.
2. "Introduction," Flannery O'Connor, *Everything That Rises Must Converge,* p. xxxiii.

quality is lost and the name becomes foolish: for instance, when a child mindlessly repeats the word time
and again, the sound itself becomes strange and funny
in its absurdity. The quality of rightness and reverence
is lost also when the name sharply contrasts with the
nature of the object to which it is attached or when the
name suggests inappropriate associations. Thus Flannery O'Connor is able to use proper names to arouse
laughter. She dated one letter to Richard Stern, "Hoover's Birthday 1959," and in the letter itself took delight
in the comic possibilities of Mystic, Connecticut.[3] Similarly, in "A Stroke of Good Fortune," Bill Hill's sales
line, Miracle Products, comically evokes a world in
which *miracle* refers to the efficiency of a banal house-
hold gadget; by contrast, Bill's wife, Ruby, considers
her pregnancy not miraculous at all, but odious. CCC
Snuff, 666, Coca-Cola (sometimes represented phoneti-
cally as Co-Cola) are named and startle the reader
because their familiarity and homeliness seem out of
place in a fictional reality charged with meaning. Place
names, such as the catalogue mentioned by Mr. Shiftlet in "The Life You Save May Be Your Own," are
often chosen for their proposterousness: Tarwater, Tennessee; Singleberry, Georgia; Lucy, Alabama; Toola-
falls, Mississippi. Such names are not really uncommon
and not innately humorous, but when they are cited in
O'Connor's stories, they become so because there is in
them a strong sense of the disparity between the place
name as a curious word and the place name as the

3. Richard Stern, "Flannery O'Connor: A Remembrance and
Some Letters," *Shenandoah,* XVI (Winter 1965), 7.

location of life and being. Thus the name is rendered ludicrous.

The names of characters, too, are often carefully selected to exemplify man's mindlessness in designating things. In "Good Country People" Mrs. Freeman's daughters are named Glynese and Carramae; in "A Good Man Is Hard to Find," Edgar Atkins Teagarden leaves his initials, E.A.T., on a watermelon for his girl friend; in the same story, the manager of the Tower restaurant is Red Sammy Butts; Hoover Shoats is in *Wise Blood;* and the twin boys in "A Temple of the Holy Ghost" are Wendell and Cory Wilkins. In two instances such onomastic horror is compounded: Sarah Ham changes her name to Star Drake in "The Comforts of Home," and Joy Hopewell in "Good Country People" changes hers to Hulga.

The delightfully comic occurrences in Flannery O'Connor's work are surprisingly numerous, but the brevity of this humor is in itself consistent with the fleeting quality of such experience in the actual world. A story as severe as "The Displaced Person" includes several truly laughable scenes, such as the one in which Mrs. Shortley draws herself up when Mr. Guizac kisses Mrs. McIntyre's hand; Mrs. Shortley is confident that her husband, Chancey, would never do such a thing: "He didn't have time to mess around."[4] Their curious show of affection for each other provides one of the funniest scenes in any of the stories. It occurs when Mr. Shortley is surreptitiously smoking in the dairy barn

4. Flannery O'Connor, *A Good Man Is Hard to Find,* p. 199. Further quotations from this work will be identified with the abbreviation *Good Man* and a page number in parentheses.

while his wife warns him of Mrs. McIntyre's rules against it:

> Mr. Shortley, without appearing to give the feat any consideration, lifted the cigarette stub with the sharp end of his tongue, drew it into his mouth, closed his lips tightly, rose, stepped out, gave his wife a good round appreciative stare, and spit the smoldering butt into the grass.
>
> "Aw Chancey," she said, "haw, haw," and she dug a little hole for it with her toe and covered it up. This trick of Mr. Shortley's was actually his way of making love to her. When he had done his courting, he had not brought a guitar to strum or anything pretty for her to keep, but had sat on her porch steps, not saying a word, imitating a paralyzed man propped up to enjoy a cigarette. When the cigarette got the proper size, he would turn his eyes to her and open his mouth and draw in the butt and then sit there as if he had swallowed it, looking at her with the most loving look anybody could imagine. It nearly drove her wild and every time he did it, she wanted to pull his hat down over his eyes and hug him to death (*Good Man*, pp. 205–206) .

The range of outright humor is broad, and a catalogue would be extensive. One can only suggest its diversity: one-hundred-year-old General Sash's perpetual exclamations about "pretty guls" and the "preemy" in Atlanta (obviously referring to the opening of *Gone With the Wind*) ; O. E. Parker, at his mother's request, having her name, Betty Jean, tattooed inside a heart; a popcorn boy admiring Enoch Emery's change purse and exclaiming, "That thang looks like a hawg bladder";[5] Glynese Freeman having a sty cured by a chiropractic student who pops her neck while she lies on the back

5. Flannery O'Connor, *Wise Blood*, p. 136. Further quotations from this work will be identified with the abbreviation *WB* and a page number in parentheses.

seat of a " '55 Mercury"; a hungry boy refusing a sandwich because he "wouldn't eat nothing bald-headed like
a guinea" (*Good Man,* p. 141) ; and Mrs. Shortley's
empathy with the distinguished bearded man on a cal-
endar, holding a bottle of patent medicine and saying,
"I have been made regular by this marvelous discovery!" (*Good Man,* p. 219).

Wise Blood abounds in such humor, and any reader
who ignores it is left with an incomplete response to the
book. Flannery O'Connor says that it is a comic novel
that "was written with zest and, if possible, . . . should
be read that way" (*WB,* p. 5). Much of the humor
stems from the rigidity and the stiff dignity of the central character, Hazel Motes. Haze is not a comic figure
per se, except in the sense that Don Quixote is—the
humor residing in the disparity between his image of
himself and the objective view presented to the reader.
His experiences with Enoch, Mrs. Watts, Sabbath, and
numerous minor characters are often humorous, but
the most consistent strain of humor is associated with
his Essex, an ancient and dilapidated automobile. That
it symbolizes his soul does not diminish the humor but
increases it. His pride in the Essex is forever betrayed;
it fails him when he most needs it to pursue his blasphemous intent.

If Haze Motes may be compared to Don Quixote, his
Sancho Panza is Enoch Emery; he is a thoroughly ridiculous country bumpkin in town, forever exposing his
naiveté, gullibility, and the perverse practicality which
he believes is the sign of wise blood. He is taken in by a
street hawker, offers ludicrous credentials to be Haze's
guide in the city, and professes to know everything

about Jesus because he has been to Rodemill Boys'
Bible Academy. His absurdity often consists of a mixture of false profundity and childishness, frequently in
juxtaposition with Haze's stern and resolute nature.
Among the funniest and yet most significant scenes in
which Enoch participates are those in which he attempts to ingratiate himself with Gonga, a gorilla man-
nequin entertaining children at the box office of a
theater. After the man curses Enoch, the boy gets his
revenge by overpowering the show people after their
performance, stealing the gorilla suit, thus imbruting
himself in it. The spectacle is humorous, but its meaning is in its pathos.

Enoch Emery is the most fully developed character of
a type found extensively in Flannery O'Connor's work
—the bumpkin whose ignorance when he is placed in
situations that outstrip his limited intelligence is humorous. Mr. Head and Nelson in "The Artificial Nigger" are of this type, and one of the many instances of
humor in that story occurs when Mr. Head conducts
Nelson on a tour of the train and shows him the men's
toilet as if it were a marvel of modern engineering; in
Atlanta Mr. Head astutely analyzes the error of the
penny-scales in giving Nelson's weight as ninety-eight
pounds: "the machine had probably printed the number upsidedown, meaning the 9 for a 6" (*Good Man*, p.
115). Chancey Shortley fits the mold too in his analysis
of the threat posed by foreigners: "about half of them
know the English language. That's where we make our
mistake, . . . —letting all them people onto English"
(*Good Man*, p. 248). Sarah Ruth Cates Parker is also
ignorant; when she tells O. E. that her favorite tattoo is

the chicken, she is referring to a red and blue representation of the national eagle. Laughable ignorance from this sort of character occurs in many of the stories and in both novels.

A major comic type is the fatuous sage who faithfully believes his trite aphorisms constitute reasonable solutions to all problems. Such characters are comic only in their folly, for they usually suffer as a result of their oversimplified understanding of complex problems. Although moral issues are easily identifiable in her fiction, Flannery O'Connor rarely draws lines which sharply distinguish good from bad, right from wrong, beautiful from ugly. She is keenly aware that the mysterious flux of life generates a complexity of such depth that its meaning is clear only to God. When her characters have the temerity to pronounce their easy answers, they demonstrate their own folly; when their confidence in their answers is boundless and their volubility in offering them extreme, the characters become comic. Such characters are, of course, the object of satire, but humor is a by-product of it. In "Good Country People" Mrs. Hopewell and Mrs. Freeman, both of them prone to shallow aphorisms, engage in veritable duels of platitude. Mrs. Hopewell achieves great heights of banality and probably compresses more triteness into a few words than any other character:

"Why!" she cried, "good country people are the salt of the earth! Besides, we all have different ways of doing, it takes all kinds to make the world go 'round. That's life!" (*Good Man*, p. 179).

Mrs. May, Mrs. Turpin, Mrs. Cope, Julian's mother, Mrs. McIntyre, and the grandmother in "A Good Man

Is Hard to Find" all belong to the type in varying degrees; Mr. Shiftlet with his searching questions and mundane, trite answers about the nature of man is a masculine example.

Mason Tarwater represents a third comic type; Sumner J. Ferris considers his "monomania for kidnapping and baptizing his infant male relatives . . . particularly funny," contending quite correctly that "comic incongruities rather add to than detract from her seriousness."[6] Regardless of the predominantly sympathetic use of Mason in the thematic structure of *The Violent Bear It Away,* he is, as Rayber maintains in his magazine article, a vanishing type whose religious fervor, in Miss O'Connor's view, is unfortunately disappearing; but she is not so narrow a writer as to present such a figure without depicting the humor of his outrageous mode of expression and his quaint ways—such as his education of his great-nephew:

His uncle had taught him Figures, Reading, Writing, and History beginning with Adam expelled from the Garden and going on down through the presidents to Herbert Hoover and on in speculation toward the Second Coming and the Day of Judgment.[7]

In an attempt to circumvent the entailment of the family property at Powderhead so that a fool (his nephew Rayber) will not inherit it, Mason goes to the city and laughably blusters from one incredulous lawyer to an-

6. "The Outside and the Inside: Flannery O'Connor's *The Violent Bear It Away,*" *Critique,* III (Winter-Spring, 1960), 12.

7. Flannery O'Connor, *The Violent Bear It Away,* p. 4. Further quotations from this work will be identified with the abbreviation *Violent* and a page number in parentheses.

other, unable to break the inviolability of a will on grounds which he considers perfectly moral and justifiable. His prophesying, as profound as it is in meaning, is amusing to Tarwater and the reader, but execrable to Rayber, his wife, and the staff of the mental institution where they place him. Having learned after four years not to prophesy on the psychiatric ward, he is released and thereafter "proceeded about the Lord's business like an experienced crook" (*Violent*, p. 62). Fleeing from Rayber's house after discovering the magazine article about him, he kidnaps his great-nephew and, as a testament to his motives, leaves the magazine in the crib where the baby had been.

When religion is the subject of humor, as Flannery O'Connor frequently makes it, one is led to conclude that she is employing a technique that allows her to write about specifically religious experiences without risking sentimentality and mawkishness. A scene in which characters go to church, for example, could become an embarrassing one if handled without great skill. Flannery O'Connor employs humor frequently in such situations. In "A Temple of the Holy Ghost" the child from whose point of view the story is told resents being forced to attend benediction by "a big moon-faced nun" of the kind that kissed "even homely children": "You put your foot in their door and they got you praying" (*Good Man*, p. 99). The child's deep insight during benediction fuses the Host and the hermaphrodite, and in her mind she repeats the *"Tantum Ergo,"* which Joanne and Susan had earlier rendered

facetiously. Even the child's prayer is edged with
humor: " 'Hep me not to be so mean,' she began
mechanically. 'Hep me not to give her so much sass. Hep
me not to talk like I do' " (p. 100). Because the incongruity of the language and the sentiment provoking
laughter provide just the right distance from the event,
its significance to the reader is emphasized, especially
when the sentences that follow, describing the priest's
raising of the Host, return him to soberness. The account of the child's remembering to say her prayers
immediately after plotting to put "something clammy"
in Joanne and Susan's bed creates a similar effect:

The sound of the calliope coming through the window kept
her awake and she remembered that she hadn't said her
prayers and got up and knelt down and began them. She
took a running start and went through to the other side of
the Apostle's Creed and then hung by her chin on the side
of the bed, empty-minded. Her prayers, when she remembered to say them, were usually perfunctory but sometimes
when she had done something wrong or heard music or lost
something, or sometimes for no reason at all, she would be
moved to fervor and would think of Christ on the long journey to Calvary, crushed three times under the rough cross.
Her mind would stay on this a while and then get empty
and when something roused her, she would find that she
was thinking of a different thing entirely, of some dog or
some girl or something she was going to do some day (*Good
Man,* p. 95).

Thus Flannery O'Connor establishes the child's very
real piety without risking religious clichés and
sentimentality.

 Flannery O'Connor was quite aware that a great portion of her audience, to whom the sacraments are little

more than archaic idiocies, would likely misunderstand her religious subject.[8] The humorous treatment of serious religious matters may reinforce the skepticism of such readers; but Flannery O'Connor uses this technique, assuming that the humor will engage the readers' interest and hold it until the subtle truth shows through. The reader thoroughly hardened against orthodox belief will not be affected even then, but perhaps a few will achieve a fresh point of view broad enough to dispose them toward a sympathy for the religious view of life. In *The Violent Bear It Away,* for example, baptism, the initial Christian sacrament and the one which dominates the novel, is the subject of humor on several occasions. Mason has to skulk to baptize the infant Tarwater; he waits until Rayber leaves the room and performs the rite with the materials at hand:

When [Rayber] came back in a few minutes, his uncle was holding Tarwater in one hand and with the other he was pouring water over his head out of the bottle that had been on the table by the crib. He had pulled off the nipple and stuck it in his pocket. He was just finishing the words of baptism as the schoolteacher came back in the door and he had had to laugh when he looked up and saw his nephew's face. It looked hacked, the old man said. Not even angry at first, just hacked (*Violent,* p. 72) .

Young Tarwater's reaction to his great-uncle's account of this incident adds more humor:

"And what did I do?" Tarwater asked.
"You didn't do nothing," the old man said as if what he did or didn't do was of no consequence whatsoever.

8. Letter from Flannery O'Connor to Andrew Lytle, February, 4, 1960, Tennessee State Library and Archives, Nashville, Tennessee.

"It was me that was the prophet," the boy said sullenly.

"You didn't even know what was going on," his uncle said.

"Oh yes I did," the child said. "I was laying there thinking" (p. 74).

Later in the novel, Bishop's affinity for water causes laughter while pointing out that one of man's most elemental urges is his impulse toward the cleansing of his spirit; whenever Bishop sees water enough to stand in, he shouts joyfully and runs toward it with his arms flapping. Similarly, in "Judgement Day" the event symbolizing physical resurrection is portrayed more humorously than any other in the story; the reader's realization that laughter is simultaneous with the accomplishment of the profound Christian theme enhances his appreciation of both the humor and the theme.

Even the mockery of religion and its general abuse are often funny, allowing the skeptical reader more opportunities for misinterpretation. As John Hawkes's article "Flannery O'Connor's Devil" demonstrates, these elements can lead even the experienced critic to believe that the author is—perhaps subconsciously—the devil's advocate. Quite the contrary, Flannery O'Connor portrays the skeptic's position humorously so that the laughter reveals his folly. In "Parker's Back" one laughs when the tattoo artist matter-of-factly inquires whether Parker wants "Father, Son or Spirit" (*Everything*, p. 234) on his back; this question is totally practical, and its complete lack of religious content is funny in the Christian context. While the tattoo artist's callousness is humorous, it serves to emphasize rather than diminish O. E.'s very real sentiments.

Another reason for the humorous representation of cynicism and disbelief is that they constitute a significant aspect of reality and can be as laughable as they are disheartening; the taxi driver who takes Hazel Motes to an address which he knows to be that of a prostitute believes Haze is a preacher and conducts a wryly humorous repartee with his passenger to assure him that he understands. Later Haze goes to a house of prostitution with a "Lapsed Catholic" (*WB*, p. 147), who knows what a mortal sin is, believes in it, but prefers to take the risks for the sake of his pleasure in it. In *The Violent Bear It Away*, the devil's most humorous lines occur when he mocks religion; he delights in pointing out to Tarwater that his uncle was the only prophet he knew who also made moonshine whiskey; later the voice jeers at Tarwater, "Lemme hear you prophesy something" (p. 38). Both of these examples reveal the silliness of a shallow, pedestrian attitude toward religious commitment; parallel actions would be to deny St. Paul's sanctity because of the thorn in his flesh or to request Moses to ask the burning bush a few questions.

Blasphemy itself is not skirted in Flannery O'Connor's work. It is often so outlandish, however, that it is funny; the reader does not take the blasphemy seriously, even when the character himself is quite earnest. Hazel Motes is a rich source of such humor: "What do I need with Jesus?" he asks. "I got Leora Watts" (*WB*, p. 56). He tells a truckdriver, "Jesus is a trick on niggers" (p. 76). The boy at the used car lot where Haze buys his Essex spouts an endless stream of blasphemy and profanity which offends even Hazel

Motes; the boy's father tells Haze that his son curses so much because something is wrong with him and in the next moment turns on the boy and says, "Goddam you, . . . quit jumping at us thataway. Keep your butt on the board" (p. 72).

The religious ignorance upon which much of this humor depends is summed up in a letter to Sabbath Lily Hawks from Mary Brittle, a newspaper columnist who offers solutions to her reader's problems:

Dear Sabbath, Light necking is acceptable, but I think your real problem is one of adjustment to the modern world. Perhaps you ought to re-examine your religious values to see if they meet your needs in Life. A religious experience can be a beautiful addition to living if you put it in the proper perspective and do not let it warf you. Read some books on Ethnical Culture (*WB*, p. 119).

The characters who have been wise enough to avoid being warped by religion are the very ones whose shallowness makes them ludicrously funny to those who believe strongly enough to be changed by the imperatives of Christianity.

Of course, even the devout are ludicrous when they are seen *sub specie aeternitatis*, and Flannery O'Connor's humor often places man in this context. Man's pride and his pretensions vanish when he appears ludicrously inadequate to cope with the demands of life, when he attempts to accomplish more than he can, and when he is "hoist with his own petar." Humor of this kind in O'Connor's work is rarely excremental, but it bears kinship with the moment in *Gulliver's Travels* when Gulliver, bent on satisfying himself that even among giants he is capable of extraordinary feats, attempts to leap across an expanse of fresh cow dung and lands in it up to his waist. In "A Late Encounter with the Enemy," Sally Poker Sash undergoes such an experience. For the premiere in Atlanta, where she must appear on stage with General Sash, she buys "a long black crepe dinner dress with a rhinestone buckle and a bolero—and a pair of silver slippers to wear with it" (*Good Man*, p. 159). She is given a corsage made of "gladiola petals taken off and painted gold and put back together to look like a rose" (p. 158), is called for by a limousine and escorted to her seat. Her deflation comes after she is on the stage and in the spotlight:

> [General Sash's remarks were] met with a great din of spontaneous applause and it was at just that instant that Sally Poker looked down at her feet and discovered that in the excitement of getting ready she had forgotten to change her shoes: two brown Girl Scout oxfords protruded from the bottom of her dress. She gave the General a yank and almost ran with him off the stage (p. 161).

Similarly, Asbury Fox in "The Enduring Chill" dramatizes his impending death and languishes, romantically relishing the consternation which he hopes the great event will generate; his condition is diagnosed not by an eminent specialist but by Dr. Block, a seedy country physician, and when Asbury gets the news, the doctor tells him, "Undulant fever ain't so bad, Azzbury. . . . It's the same as Bang's in a cow" (*Everything*, p. 113). As a result, Asbury suddenly sees his own ridiculousness and quickly retrieves the key to his literary leavings that would have exposed his immature nonsense to his mother and sister. The laughter at Sally Poker and Asbury is not scornful, for it is directed at the pitiful universal imperfection of man; it is like the cosmic laughter of Chaucer's Troilus after he has assumed a vantage point from the seventh sphere and can see the humor of his own behavior and that of men in general. Flannery O'Connor's readers are transported to such a vantage point by her persistently Christian theme; through her humor they can look down upon man as Troilus did.

In *The Violent Bear It Away,* Rayber's great confidence in reason often puts him into situations that diminish him comically. On one occasion he follows when Tarwater leaves the house at night; his self-important role of protector and moral guide leads him into a series of experiences that reveal, not the limits of his reason, but the pitiful, though laughable, limits of his humanness. Leaving the house in a hurry, he puts his suit on over pajamas and forgets to wear shoes; Tarwater walks so fast that Rayber has difficulty keeping up:

> Rayber felt the accelerated beat of his heart. He took a handkerchief out of his pocket and wiped his forehead and inside the neck of his pajama top. He walked over something sticky on the sidewalk and shifted hurriedly to the other side, cursing under his breath (*Violent,* p. 120).

People stare at him as if he were an escaped lunatic or a lost and stumbling alcoholic, and children in front of a theater jeer at him. His wrath, chagrin, and embarrassment fail to deter him. Still in the name of a noble purpose, he stumbles in a dark alley:

> A garbage can materialized in his path. There was a noise like the collapse of a tin house and he found himself sitting up with his hand and one foot in something unidentifiable.

He scrambled up and limped on, hearing his own curses like the voice of a stranger broadcast through his hearing aid (p. 123).

Flannery O'Connor's point in making Rayber laughable in this manner is quite clear; his mission of secular conversion is not only as funny as his uncle's monomania to baptize—but is so ludicrously carried out that it leads him into a wasteland of dark alleys, garbage cans, and unidentifiable filth.

Only a fine line distinguishes Rayber's misfortunes from others which can be construed only as grim humor; these are occurrences which occasion laughter at people in their most wretched condition—not when they are the victims of their own folly, but when they are victims of the ravages of mental and physical illness or deformity, and when they confront violence, death, and tragedy.

The gamut of grim humor is broad, for it ranges from indirect mention of horror to openly dramatized scenes. In "The Displaced Person" a fleeting moment of humor appears when Mr. Shortley suggests to Sulk that he go back to Africa. " 'I ain't goin there,' the boy said. 'They might eat me up' " (*Good Man*, p. 247). The Negro's reply is reminiscent of cartoons showing two missionaries in a boiling pot surrounded by natives; although Sulk is half-whimsical and the cartoon is patently a humorous cliché, the fact remains that the image in both is that of an extremely revolting actuality, cannibalism. It is laughable only because of the point of view from which it is seen; in Sulk's remark and the cartoon only a slight sense of horror and only an insignificant degree of seriousness are apparent. More of both is found in the following passage from *Wise Blood,* in which Enoch Emery explains to Hazel Motes how he escaped from the woman who adopted him:

After a second he said, "I scared hell out of that woman, that's how. I studied on it and studied on it. I even prayed. I said, 'Jesus, show me the way to get out of here without killing thisyer woman and getting sent to the penitentiary,' and durn if He didn't. I got up one morning at just daylight and I went in her room without my pants on and pulled the sheet off her and giver a heart attact. Then I went back to my daddy and we ain't seen hide of her since (*WB,* p. 48).

As humorous as the incident is to Enoch and momentarily to the reader, he is aware of the genuine fear and shock suffered by the woman. He may feel that a person as perverted as Enoch is actually capable of considering murder or carrying out the mock rape. The generally comic nature of the novel dictates the humor in this instance: Enoch is the principal comic figure in *Wise Blood* and must be developed consistently within that role. The serious thematic points relating to his character must be rendered through the comic texture, just as Falstaff's highly important thematic function in *Henry IV* is accomplished without sacrificing his comic role—for example, Falstaff's account of mutilating Hotspur's corpse.

The mixture of the comic and the tragic in Flannery O'Connor's fiction frequently occurs when feeble-mindedness is the subject. In *The Violent Bear It Away,*

Mason Tarwater does not want his great-nephew to attend public school and prepares a scheme that will keep him at home in Powderhead. When the truant officer arrives, the boy makes a great show of being demented, and the horrified truant officer decides to leave him at home in peace:

> "I speck he better stay at home," the officer said. "I wouldn't want to put a strain on him," and he commenced to speak of other things (*Violent*, p. 18).

This scene is funny, but, taken out of context, shocking in that it seems to mock the simulated condition. Its purpose in the novel, however, is to suggest the lengths to which Mason Tarwater will go to protect his great-nephew from the corrupt teachings of the George Raybers of the world. It is connected too with the significance of Bishop's feeble-mindedness, which old Mason construed as God's way of protecting the boy from Rayber's godlessness. By implication, Tarwater would be better off an idiot than a disciple of Rayber. In William Faulkner's *The Hamlet,* an extraordinary amount of grim humor concerns the idiot Ike Snopes, who is, because of his condition, the only Snopes who is not damned by the ravenous immorality of his family. Like the humor about Ike, the humor involving Bishop Rayber points up his innocence more than it creates pathos. For instance, when Rayber, Tarwater, and Bishop are eating at the Cherokee Lodge, the dancing of a group of vulgar adolescents fascinates Bishop; he sets up a furious commotion when they stop. As an infant is attracted by rattles and bright colors, Bishop is charmed by the color, the motion, and the noise of the dancers. But his presence is like the eye of God scrutinizing the preposterous antics of the dancers until they flee in discomfort. There are two reasons for laughter in this scene: Bishop's shattering interruption of the composure of everyone in the dining room, and the irony that Bishop, the idiot, triumphs over those who are "normal."

Thematically the idiot also triumphs in "The Life You Save May Be Your Own"; Lucynell Crater's behavior is humorous because she is congenitally immune to the immoral machinations of Mr. Shiftlet. Throughout his cultivation of her and her stupid mother, one has the feeling that her hilarious antics mysteriously mock the purposes of both of them and that her idiocy is a blessed condition far superior to their calculating devices. Mr. Shiftlet teaches Lucynell, who is "completely deaf and had never said a word in her life" (*Good Man*, p. 59), to say *bird* and thereafter "The big rosy-faced girl followed him everywhere, saying 'Burrttdt ddbirrrttdt,' and clapping her hands" (p. 59). She attends him even while he tries to repair the coveted automobile:

Late in the afternoon, terrible noises issued from the shed and the old woman rushed out of the house, thinking Lucynell was somewhere having a fit. Lucynell was sitting on a chicken crate, stamping her feet and screaming, "Burrddttt! bddurrddtttt!" but her fuss was drowned out by the car. With a volley of blasts it emerged from the shed, moving in a fierce and stately way. Mr. Shiftlet was in the driver's seat, sitting very erect. He had an expression of serious modesty on his face as if he had just raised the dead (p. 61).

As comic a scene as this requires a long pause. From a clinical standpoint it is grotesque if for no other reason than that its participants are a one-armed man and a woman with the mentality of a five-year-old. Mr. Shiftlet, after marrying Lucynell and getting temporary possession of the car, is further harassed by her simpleness:

> Occasionally he stopped his thoughts long enough to look at Lucynell in the seat beside him. She had eaten the lunch as soon as they were out of the yard and now she was pulling the cherries off the hat one by one and throwing them out the window. He became depressed in spite of the car (p. 65).

Even when he leaves her snoring on the counter of the Hot Spot, she is clearly his superior, and the laughter at her is one measure of Mr. Shiftlet's moral defeat.

The grotesqueness of illness and deformity can sometimes provide humor, but it is rarely gratuitous. Usually some significant connection with the theme can be pointed out (as certain features of a religious nature are) by humor more effectively and more convincingly than through more sedate techniques. Humor of this sort appears in "A Circle in the Fire" in Mrs. Pritchard's excessive interest in a woman who conceived a child and gave birth to it in an iron lung. In "Good Country People" one cannot help laughing at Mrs. Freeman's interest in Hulga's artificial leg and the woman's general preoccupation with such things; she "had a special fondness for the details of secret infections, hidden deformities, assaults upon children. Of diseases, she preferred the lingering or incurable" (*Good Man,* p. 174). The humor in this trait depends in part upon the reader's shocked recognition of a quite ordinary morbidity rarely revealed by the distance provided by fiction. But the humor of Mrs. Freeman's relatively innocent curiosity does not exist in a vacuum; its counterpart occurs in the predatory curiosity of the Bible salesman when he insists upon examining Hulga's stump and finally steals her glasses and her artificial leg.

Death itself is as common in Flannery O'Connor's stories as it is in the world; it frequently yields much of the painful laughter in her work. Unless one is to consider the writer a misanthrope or a literary sadist, he must find good reasons for an incitement to laughter in the midst of a scene depicting death; several examples from Flannery O'Connor's work demonstrate the artistic validity of her technique. In "The Displaced Person," Mrs. Shortley's death takes place in the family car, which is bursting with Shortley possessions, as the family leaves Mrs. McIntyre's farm for good:

She suddenly grabbed Mr. Shortley's elbow and Sarah Mae's foot at the same time and began to tug and pull on them as if she were trying to fit the two extra limbs onto herself. Mr. Shortley began to curse and quickly stopped the car and Sarah Mae yelled to quit but Mrs. Shortley apparently intended to rearrange the whole car at once. She thrashed forward and backward, clutching at everything she could get her hands on and hugging it to herself, Mr. Shortley's head, Sarah Mae's leg, the cat, a wad of white bedding, her own big moon-like knee; then all at once her fierce expression faded into a look of astonishment and her grip on what she had loosened. One of her eyes drew near to the other and seemed to collapse quietly and she was still.
. . . [The two girls] didn't know that she had had a great

experience or ever been displaced in the world from all that
belonged to her (*Good Man,* pp. 222–223) .

The catalogue, "Mr. Shortley's head, Sarah Mae's leg,
the cat, a wad of white bedding, her own big moon-like
knee" inspires ironic laughter. In the first place, there is
macabre humor in the irony that these details are similar to Mrs. Shortley's ignorant associations regarding
the image of a mound of European Jews exterminated
by the Nazis. Second, and this is perhaps a sounder
justification for the humor, Mrs. Shortley cannot pass
mildly away as virtuous men do; she struggles against
death, grasping at everything within reach as if to preserve life by holding on to material things—somewhat
in the manner of Everyman in the medieval morality
play. The shabby, worn, and pathetic objects for which
she grasps demonstrate ludicrously the vanity of possessions in this imperfect world. Mrs. Shortley does not
understand life and death in the Christian context, and
her ignorance and fear are humorous from a cosmic,
Christian vantage point.

Unlike Mrs. Shortley, Mason Tarwater is thoroughly
prepared for his death, and his open display of familiarity and confidence regarding it assures the reader that
laughter over an ostensibly sorrowful occasion is perfectly in order. He builds his own coffin, keeps it on the
back porch, and lies in it while instructing Tarwater
about his burial. He implores the boy to roll him into
the grave if using the box is not feasible, but by no
means to let the dogs nudge him into the grave before
the hole is deep enough. When Mason dies at the breakfast table, Tarwater finishes eating and finally says,
"Just hold your horses. I already told you I would do it

right" (*Violent,* pp. 13–14). He does not, of course, but Buford Munson does, finishing the grave where the boy started it, "under the fig tree because the old man would be good for the figs" (p. 22).

Similarly in *Wise Blood,* deaths, even the extremely shocking ones, are tinged with humor. Hazel Motes dreams of his father's burial:

> He saw him humped over on his hands and knees in his coffin, being carried that way to the graveyard. "If I can keep my can in the air," he heard the old man say, "nobody can shut nothing on me," but when they got his box to the hole, they let it drop down with a thud and his father flattened out like anybody else (*WB,* p. 20).

This dream could be made sober rather than funny, but it would then contribute little to the comic quality of the novel and would be inconsistent with the outlandish nature of Haze's imagination. Further, laughter is in order here, as in Mrs. Shortley's death, because Haze at this point foolishly fails to think beyond the grave.

By the time of his own death, however, Haze has changed sufficiently to be contemptuous of death. He tells the policemen who find him dying in a ditch, "I want to go on where I'm going" (p. 230), and as if to oblige him, one of the novice policemen "hit him over the head with his new billy" (p. 231), his sadism a classic example of grim humor, the many examples of which in Flannery O'Connor's work are usually redeemed by her Christian theme. Robert Fitzgerald has remarked that the presence of humor in some of Flannery O'Connor's most tragic scenes is "like the presence of grace"; and one must agree with his further suggestion that because of the convergence of humor and horror, her work may be considered generically as tragi-comedy, the most Christian of *genres.*[9]

There are, of course, various types of humor and various purposes for it. The most literal kind is some-times akin to local color, but for the most part this simple humor is a relishing of the lighter foibles and blind spots of mankind; it is good natured. A somewhat deeper significance is apparent in humor arising from characters who in other contexts of the stories reveal moral culpability in the very areas that produced laugh-ter at other times; such comic incongruities indicate Miss O'Connor's recognition of the complexity of human response, and they serve to heighten the serious-ness of her intent rather than to diminish or destroy it. Humor is often used to express religious themes and religious situations without sentimentality or obvious didacticism; and just as humor provides distance from religion to achieve a sympathetic response to it, so is humor used to establish a distance from blasphemy and atheism to demonstrate its narrow and sometimes ludi-crous dialectic. And in nearly all of this humor, there is the theme of man's triviality when he appears against the background of eternity.

Such a Christian perspective informs most of the humor arising from idiocy, death, and suffering, which can be humorous only if one can see through them to truths that render them insignificant and fleeting. Grim humor, then, is one of Flannery O'Connor's devices to open a window through which one can see the true country, and her comic humor is a good-natured and objective means of enjoying the countryside.

9. *Op. cit.,* p. xxxiii.

Chapter 8 Technique as Theme: Satire and Irony

ON more than one oc-
casion, Flannery O'Connor remarked that her work was
not understood. She knew that one reason for the lack
of understanding was the essentially secular viewpoint
of many readers, but she was equally aware that even
devout Christians were often perplexed or mistaken
about the meaning of her stories and novels. In a letter
to Robert Fitzgerald she complained good-naturedly of
having to explain *Wise Blood* to one of her uncompre-
hending relatives:

> My current literary assignment (from Regina) [her
> mother] is to write an introduction for Cousin Katie "so she
> won't be shocked," to be *pasted* on the inside of her book.
> This piece has to be in the tone of the Sacred Heart Messen-
> ger and carry the burden of contemporary critical thought.
> I keep putting it off.[1]

Cousin Katie's inability to understand has nothing to
do with a lack of sympathy for the theme of the work, if

1. Robert Fitzgerald, "Introduction," Flannery O'Connor,
Everything That Rises Must Converge, p. xix.

she could only read through to it; instead, Cousin Katie does not know how to approach a piece of modern literature and would have as much trouble with Joseph Conrad, T. S. Eliot, or William Faulkner. She represents Flannery O'Connor's local counterpart to the little old lady in Dubuque, the archetype of those who expect fiction to be beautiful and uplifting.

To anyone really sophisticated about literature and its techniques, T. S. Eliot's famous comparison of a sunset to a patient etherized upon a table was really nothing very new; yet more than forty years after that landmark in literature, supposedly skilled readers continue to react to such techniques in the fashion of cousin Katie and the lady from Dubuque. Jesse Hill Ford, for example, says: "Reading Miss O'Connor closely, one suspects that she hated humankind in general. . . . She dealt in black humor. Her fiction has an ax-murder feel to it."[2] On the contrary, one could entertain such a suspicion only if he failed to read deeply. As previous chapters have shown, Miss O'Connor's vision is forever focused upon Christian themes, particularly the presence of grace which—recognized or ignored—is the sign of a principle of love or Christian charity in the universe. That Flannery O'Connor's talent disposed her to indicate her faith in charity by portraying the neglect and abuse of it by no means gives occasion to interpret her as a misanthrope. For many years Swift was misunderstood by some critics in much the same fashion, whereas recent criticism has discerned the real inten-

2. "Vanderbilt's Literary Symposium: Program for Spectators," Nashville *Tennessean,* September 4, 1966, B-1.

tion of his work. The following remarks by Bonamy Dobrée are about Swift, but they could apply quite well to Flannery O'Connor:

[His work] is not a reviling of man's indignity, but a passionate plea for the dignity of man, in spite of his loathsome body, his absurd mind, his ridiculous political pretensions, his arrogant ignorance. The only hope of salvation, Swift tells us, is to rid ourselves of our cruel illusions, to be aware of, and to accept the hells beneath, so that we may not subside into them.[3]

Like Swift, Flannery O'Connor was moved by a savage indignation that man so often failed to achieve, or even strive for, the reason and charity he is capable of. And like him, she resorted to shocking, violent methods and subject matter, incurring the risk of being misunderstood. Her use of grotesque characters and situations and her frequent inclusion of grim humor are technical features as well as aspects of her Christian theme.

The difficulties of interpretation are not, however, limited to the high incidence of shocking details; other apparently negative features of her fiction aggravate the notion that Flannery O'Connor is a destructive malcontent. Not only does a grotesque reality preoccupy her; she is also a satirist with biting skill. Satire does not, of course, carry her most profound themes, but it is adjunct to them, attacking through mockery various follies which lie on the periphery of tragedy. The pride of intellectuals is mocked throughout her work. For example, Asbury Fox's ambitious dreams of Art, his affected liberalism, his pretentious interest in James Joyce, and

3. *English Literature in the Early Eighteenth Century, 1700–1740*, p. 460.

his narrow contempt for his rural home all pale before the threat of death and the firm rebuke of the priest. Other intellectuals are similarly dealt with: Hulga Hopewell in "Good Country People," Julian in "Everything That Rises Must Converge," Mary Grace in "Revelation," Thomas in "The Comforts of Home," and Calhoun and Mary Elizabeth in "The Partridge Festival." Although none of these stories is chiefly satirical in a narrow sense, all exhibit the mockery suggesting the limits of man's reason.

The sociologist and the schoolteacher are satirical types closely akin to the intellectual. George Rayber in *The Violent Bear It Away* and Sheppard in "The Lame Shall Enter First" are sociologists whose occupational follies are mocked. Both of them are involved deeply enough in their respective stories to rise above caricature, but as sociologists they are satirized in that they attempt to solve highly complex human problems through oversimplified formulas of behavior. On the satirical level, Rayber is an automaton who deals with his own relatives as he would the hypothetical characters set in motion by textbook problems; and Sheppard reveals his shallowness by placing his faith in games (as City Recreation Director) and educational toys. Teachers, such as Sally Poker Sash in "A Late Encounter with the Enemy," Mary George Fox in "The Enduring Chill," and Wesley May in "Greenleaf" are consistently portrayed unfavorably—not as teachers but as examples of the deplorable chasm between the ideals and the actualities of education, particularly in the areas of human values and the old verities; the professional bearers of knowledge are often further from the truth than the illiterates. Such satire would be destructive if it were categorical, but Flannery O'Connor's scorn falls upon the specific inadequacies of the types, not upon the category. She did not hate schoolteachers and sociologists any more than she hated mankind.

Caution is also necessary when one considers other areas of satire; a reader could plausibly ask why Flannery O'Connor hated the South. He must be told that she did not, although she satirized its follies with vigor —not because its follies were southern, but because they were the ones she could observe first-hand. Ridiculous features of the southern landscape are apparent throughout her work: shabby roadside taverns, highway signs imploring drivers to get right with God, rundown farms, and a great variety of southern grotesques. While these are more properly thought of as part of the setting rather than objects of satire, there are two stories which mock institutions peculiarly associated with the South: "A Late Encounter with the Enemy" and "The Partridge Festival." The first of these uses George Poker Sash, an ugly, senile, moribund veteran of the Confederate Army who is interested only in "pretty guls" and cannot remember his experiences in the Civil War to satirize shallow glorification of the past. The old man's granddaughter, Sally Poker Sash, has no genuine understanding of the past; she abuses it by attempting to elevate herself through identification with her grandfather. Graduating from college after twenty years of summer school, Sally Poker insists that the old man be on the commencement platform as a dignitary; through this device she intends to show *them* what she stands for:

This *them* was not anybody in particular. It was just all the upstarts who had turned the world on its head and unsettled the ways of decent living.

She meant to stand on that platform in August with the General sitting in his wheel chair on the stage behind her and she meant to hold her head very high as if she were saying, "See him! See him! My kin, all you upstarts! Glorious upright old man standing for the old traditions! Dignity! Honor! Courage! See him!"[4]

The true dignity which invests the past is defiled by the woman's deplorable vulgarity and foolish pride. The theme of this satire is broadened considerably by the inclusion of flashbacks of the events which altered the old man's past to feed the puerile vanity of the present. George Sash cannot remember whether he was a private or a captain, and yet he is presented as General Tennessee Flintrock Sash to the public attending the première of *Gone With the Wind* in Atlanta; the UDC members rise to applaud him and subsequently display him in his Hollywood general's uniform every year on Confederate Memorial Day. The satirical theme is that the South desecrates its past by perverting it for selfish reasons, public as well as private.

The satire of "The Partridge Festival" focuses upon a southern form of commercial promotion and exploitation, the azalea festival. Although the total meaning of this story is deep, its satiric texture cannot be denied. The town of Partridge is smug, self-righteous, and oriented to the shops whose proprietors profit from turn-

4. Flannery O'Connor, *A Good Man Is Hard to Find*, p. 156. Further quotations from this work will be identified with the abbreviation *Good Man* and a page number in parentheses.

ing natural beauty into trade; Natchez, Mobile, Charleston, Wilmington, and countless southern small towns are the annual sites of such promotion. Flannery O'Connor used the custom primarily for its ironic possibilities, but she uses the setting to expose hypocrisy, crass commercialism, petty small-town provincialism, and the insignificant absurdities carried out by civic clubs—in this story, arresting those who fail to buy and wear an azalea festival badge.

Satire focused upon the city and the encroachments of vulgar progressivism in the country is closely related to satire on the South. In both O'Connor novels there is a strong infusion of *ingenu* satire; it arises from the fact that both central figures, Hazel Motes and Francis Marion Tarwater, are young and almost totally innocent of the customs and characteristics of the cities into which they are thrust by events. Both boys have fierce rural dignity, moral fervor, and sharp eyes for whatever is foolish and irrational. Hazel Motes stubbornly refuses to succumb to the shallow dreams of success and urban adjustment that obsess Enoch Emery, and he indignantly rejects Hoover Shoats's cynical plans to earn a fast dollar through evangelism. Tarwater, as a child with his grandfather in Atlanta, is startled by the callousness of the people in the city. Years later Rayber conducts the boy on a tour of the city, the conventional details of which become tawdry and embarrassingly irrelevant under Tarwater's suspicious, noncommittal gaze. Searching for something "just beyond his vision" (p. 108), he is unmoved by supermarkets, municipal government, escalators, and sports cars.

Similar satiric diminution of urban landscape and

ideals may be found in "The Artificial Nigger," "The Lame Shall Enter First," and in "Everything That Rises Must Converge." The city is quite naturally associated with intellectual pride and sophistication, such as that of Asbury, Calhoun and Mary Elizabeth, and Julian.

Just as these hypocritically sophisticated characters are denizens of urban culture, so is the type represented by T. Fawcett Meeks, the copper flue salesman who drives Tarwater to the city after Mason Tarwater's death. Meeks, in all sincerity, tells Tarwater that love is an effective sales method; his wisdom, Meeks maintains, came from "The School of Experience" where he earned "the Hard Lesson from Life degree."[5] His pride in being a self-made man, his confidence in the saving grace of commercialism, and his prostitution of human emotions in the interest of Southern Copper Parts are characteristics of modern urban America that Flannery O'Connor shows are becoming increasingly apparent in the outlands, too. The city fathers of Partridge, for example, are similar to Meeks; and the coarse depredations of the country carried out by Mark Fortune and Tilman in "A View of the Woods" and Manley Pointer in "Good Country People" are other satirical portrayals of the incursions of commercialism beyond the city limits.

The central figure in "A Stroke of Good Fortune," Ruby Hill, is a type of modern woman satirized in several of the stories. Married but childless, she is proud

5. Flannery O'Connor, *The Violent Bear It Away*, pp. 59–60. Further quotations from this work will be identified with the abbreviation *Violent* and a page number in parentheses.

of having prevented conception of a child, and the story mocks her for the denial of her womanhood and for her chagrin upon learning that she is pregnant. In *The Violent Bear It Away*, Rayber's wife repudiates her role as mother to Bishop and prefers to promote the welfare of anonymous destitute children abroad; Sally Poker Sash has sacrificed marriage and maternity for a degree in elementary education. Like Ruby Hill, old Tanner's daughter in "Judgement Day" is married and childless, and she considers caring for her father "As bad as having a child."[6]

On the other hand, matrimony and motherhood are anything but exempt from satirical attack; one of Flannery O'Connor's most recurrent character types is that of the grandmother, mother, or widow who fails miserably in her domestic role. Excluding highly unsympathetic figures such as the parents in "The River," there is a long list of such characters: Mrs. May in "Greenleaf," the grandmother in "A Good Man Is Hard to Find," Mrs. Hopewell in "Good Country People," Julian's mother in "Everything That Rises Must Converge," Mrs. Fox in "The Enduring Chill," Thomas's mother in "The Comforts of Home," and Mary Grace's mother in "Revelation." In varying degrees, all of these characters are parties to a traditional conflict between generations, and they are satirized for their usually betrayed pride in their children and for expecting their children to conform to stereotyped, though alien, patterns of behavior and outlook. Such satire may not, however, be

6. Flannery O'Connor, *Everything That Rises Must Converge,* p. 248. Further quotations from this work will be identified with the abbreviation *Everything* and a page number in parentheses.

read as an end in itself; as Robert McCown has pointed out, Flannery O'Connor usually shows "compassion for those whom she satirizes."[7] The reader who finds nothing more than this minor and compassionate satire in such characterizations has missed the most significant feature of the stories in which they appear; in nearly every instance, the portrayal which seems negative if the satire alone is considered is actually extremely complex; the apparently unsympathetic character is revealed in an entirely different light at the conclusion of the story. This generalization must be applied also to the other types of satire enumerated; satire directed at intellectuals, sociologists, teachers, the South, and the city is not central to the fiction but plays a part in the ironic texture, which is a hallmark of the Flannery O'Connor technique and a very real theme in her work.

Among the various difficulties encountered in interpreting Flannery O'Connor's fiction, the most formidable is irony; yet it is an indispensable characteristic. If irony is not acknowledged and understood, one is at odds to account for apparent contradictions; he is unable to place her satire and her use of the grotesque in proper perspective, and he is left with only an incomplete sense of her Christian theme. Richard Coleman speaks of the problems of interpretation caused by irony in O'Connor's work: "Not the least mystery is that of who is the bad character, or the more evil of the two

7. "Flannery O'Connor and the Reality of Sin," *Catholic World*, CLXXXVIII (January 1959), 209.

bad ones. And where is the good?"[8] One is likely to believe that this mystery, if it has no resolution, indicates one of two things: the author is naive enough not to know the meaning of his own narrative and deliberately contrives insoluble ironies, or the author proposes that experience itself is an absurdity insofar as judgments are impossible and ironies are therefore the only sound generalizations applicable to life. Neither of these answers is the proper resolution to the perplexing ironies of Flannery O'Connor.

The rationale of her irony is threefold. First, irony is a means of achieving artistic distance from characters and situations; when an apparently unsympathetic portrayal is reversed, the resulting shock demands complete reappraisal. Miss O'Connor's devotion to a positive Christian theme accounts for her use of this indirect and complex approach; because her thematic commitment is profound and uncompromising, she refuses to rely upon conventional graying of character and draws large, shocking pictures which often depict the opposite of what their lines suggest at first glance. Whereas the gray representation fosters a linear ebb and flow of sympathy and antipathy, the bolder antithesis of ironic shock, even with the risk that the reader will refuse to reconsider, can possibly achieve a deeper reaction. This antithesis is the basis of the second reason for Miss O'Connor's irony: the choice that she wishes to dramatize is a severe one, and if a character comes to an epiphany relative to the choice, his revelation is likely

8. "Flannery O'Connor: A Scrutiny of Two Forms of Her Many-Leveled Art," *The Phoenix* [College of Charleston] (Fall-Winter 1965–66), p. 48.

to suggest sharp, ironic contrasts between what he had been and what he is at the moment of truth. This irony is basic to the Christian belief that the purifying effect of communion with Christ miraculously projects a man into a new existence, significantly different from his former identity in sin. The third reason for Miss O'Connor's irony is related to this Christian paradox. From her point of view and from the church's, it is extremely difficult to separate the good from the bad, the saved from the damned; both reason and emotion —and certainly morality as merely an aspect of outward behavior—are often at odds with faith, which may be latent, hidden, or unidentifiable. Even when faith is not apparent in the worldly context, one must hesitate to apply his conception of God's yardstick. Coleman suggests that such irony in Flannery O'Connor's fiction is not a withholding of judgment so much as a positive concern for all characters, from the vicious to the innocent.[9] Thus one can contend that Miss O'Connor's irony is not a form of Pyrrhonism but an aspect of her faith that the outwardly grotesque world is not as bad as it seems. She was not a Christian Pollyanna, nor did she philosophically apologize for rampant pride, hypocrisy, and satanism; but she did believe that these forces, while permanent in the world, are terminable in the individual, who is consequently eligible for grace to the moment after death. All of these reasons for irony may be reduced to the tension in Miss O'Connor's fiction between faith and disbelief, within a single character, between two or more characters, or between the authorial attitude and that of the audience.

9. *Ibid.*, p. 45.

In "The Partridge Festival," the irony is so extensive that the author's meaning may easily be misinterpreted. Because the story satirizes the southern town of Partridge during its azalea festival, the reader is led to expect a congruency between this satire and the theme of the story. But it is not there—not precisely, at any rate. Reading this story for the first time, however, one is easily misled; the irony basic to its technique—and to Flannery O'Connor's method generally—purposely leads the reader to draw conclusions which become invalid at the end of the story, or when the reader has reconsidered the story carefully. The reader recognizes immediately that the setting and the situation are highly satirical; he may fit into that framework the characterizations of Aunt Bessie and Aunt Mattie as extreme examples of the narrow, provincial, short-sighted morality of the town. Reinforcing such an analysis is the presence of two characters, Calhoun and Mary Elizabeth, who are members of a broader, more liberal-thinking world, that of the university; even though they are not altogether sympathetically portrayed (they are snobbish and somewhat disrespectful), they bring to the central situation an understanding which meshes perfectly with the direction of the satire: initially they take the part of the murderer Singleton against the hypocritical town of Partridge. Finally, however, they see the man as an insane murderer, and their epiphanies bring them to identify with the real Singleton and simultaneously with the people of Partridge. This is a complex irony, for if one reacts too sharply to his original wrong conclusion, he will be equally wrong in believing that Calhoun's aunts, his grandfather (who founded the azalea festival), the barber, and the Jay-

cees are, after all, on the side of God and the angels.
The truth is that Singleton is an insane murderer, but
the action itself is touched off by the festival and the
Jaycees who arrested Singleton, making them participants in his guilt; the barber intimates the indignities
Singleton has been subjected to by the town, telling
Calhoun that Singleton is a bastard and probably half
"something foreign," and that someone once put a dead
cat in his well—one of many such harassments which
the barber seems willing to list for the boy in his chair.
A further indication of the very real participation of
the town in Singleton's guilt is the comment of an old
man who, observing the funeral of one of Singleton's
victims, expresses some satisfaction that the man is
dead: "The only bullet that went right. . . . Biller was
a wastrel. Drunk at the time."[10] In effect this man callously judges Biller and sanctions his murder. Similarly,
the judgments of Calhoun and Mary Elizabeth are pre-
sumptuous and proud; what we learn finally in the
story is not that their opinions are wrong but that in
making their judgments they must judge themselves as
well as others: that their unconventionality is akin to
Singleton's madness and that they share some sympa-
thies with salesmen and Jaycees. It may be seen, then,
that the irony of the story, though complex, does finally
have a purpose, rhetorical as well as thematic; the story
does not say that the situation represented is meaningless because of its incredible complexity, but that pride
from any vantage point blinds the participant and the
observer. The only objective vantage point is that from

    10. Flannery O'Connor, "The Partridge Festival," reprinted in
The Sense of Fiction, Welker and Gower, editors, p. 377.

which the story is told, and it is only from there that one
may see the truths inherent in the situation.

Singleton, then, is a madman and an evil man, yet as
vile and revolting as he appears in the final scene of the
story, he is not an altogether unsympathetic figure. Sympathy, however, is not directed toward him because of
what he did, as Calhoun and Mary Elizabeth would
desire when they maintain that his action was that of a
courageous, independent, righteously outraged noncon-
formist. Instead, the reader feels ironic sympathy, de-
spising the man's deeds while having compassion for his
wretchedness. A quite similar situation exists in "A
Good Man Is Hard to Find." The early portions of this
story function to characterize both the grandmother
and the Misfit unsympathetically, the grandmother by
dramatic means, the Misfit indirectly by frequent reference to him by others. Both of them are unpleasant,
destructive characters, sharing in the responsibility for
the multiple killing, but the positive Christian theme is
expressed through them: the grandmother becomes
worthy by recognizing her participation in evil as the
Misfit's symbolic mother, and the Misfit is revealed as
an outrageous, shocking representative of mankind suffering and protesting against a world of injustice. The
Misfit's suffering is intense because he fails to understand it in the context of Christianity; his highly
charged colloquial dialogue with the grandmother demonstrates that he is engaged with moral questions, and
his answers, even though wrong, evoke sympathy. His
yearning for absolute authority to impose order upon
the world is indicated by his remark that the grandmother would have been a good woman "if it had been

somebody there to shoot her every minute of her life"
(*Good Man,* p. 29). He rebukes Bobby Lee for making
light of his comment and tells him, "It's no real pleasure in life" (p. 29). The Misfit, then, in juxtaposition
to a similarly destructive figure who has recognized the
reality of grace at the last minute, is a tragic figure who
struggles vainly against his own convictions. "A Good
Man Is Hard to Find," like "The Partridge Festival,"
must be understood in terms of its highly ironic pattern: the author enlists the reader's conventional sym-
pathies in one direction and then turns them the opposite way.

Although the evil aspects of the Misfit are readily
identifiable by all readers, there are many O'Connor
characters whose behavior is such that the reader accepts, even admires it, only to find that the character's
apparently good qualities are the very ones of which he
must be purged. Such irony may be seen in Mrs. May in
"Greenleaf," both Mrs. Hopewell and Hulga in "Good
Country People," and in Mrs. Turpin in "Revelation."
Mrs. May's life is outwardly shallow; it is bound up in
the petty concerns of making her dairy farm profitable,
and her chief agonies are its failures and her disappointment in her sons, Wesley and Scofield. But to state
the theme baldly is to misrepresent the total effect of the
story, and to some extent its theme. Mrs. May's weak-
nesses are in some measure the means of her strength;
one must allow that she has suffered injustices: a
widow, she has made the farm support her and her sons
only to have them mock her effort. Wesley and Scofield
are signally inferior to their mother; while she is hope-
ful, they are cynical, and while she is an industrious

manager, they are weak, unmasculine shirkers. The bull which ravages her herd, destroys her property, and finally kills her is symbolic of the injustices of the world which she suffers: the bull is not only a direct offense against her and her property but is associated with the dereliction of Mr. Greenleaf and the May sons and with the disillusioning success of E. T. and O. T. Greenleaf. Even when one recognizes that Mrs. May is duty-proud and somewhat envious of the Greenleaf twins, he must admire her for her ability to cope with the problems of this world unsentimentally and decisively. The irony in this story is not a complete reversal of one's feelings about Mrs. May, but a more subtle one. The reader realizes that his admiration of her has been for reasons that are not valid in the unfolding Christian theme, and he realizes too that in the Christian context her apparent virtues are her vices. At the conclusion of the story, however, when Mrs. May is gored by the bull, her acceptance of death and her recognition of its meaning redeem her vices. One can see then that her acceptance of death on the horns of the bull is a moment of insight in which she accepts her fate as a final injustice of the world, not different in kind from the other injustices which she has been subject to. The difference is that while she accepted the others with proud indignation, she accepts this ultimate injustice philosophically. At this point, undergoing the restoration of her sight and coming to a last discovery, she transcends the complaint of the Misfit, that he cannot make a sensible equation between his own evil nature and the punishment he has suffered. In other words, Mrs. May comes to understand the injustices of the world as an aspect of the condition of man, not as a personal affront. Unlike the Misfit, she has accepted and endured the injustices of the secular world, and her character finally is equal to the ultimate injustice of death. Her defeats in the secular world (which give the opportunity for her pride to manifest itself) prepare her for the defeat which her acceptance of it nullifies.

Because of similarly complex and subtle ironies, there is no easy analysis of the characters in "Good Country People." Hulga's pride, her disdain of her home and mother, her vanity concerning her leg, and her Ph.D. in philosophy dispose the reader to put aside any false sympathy for her because she has lost her leg as a child. On the other hand, Hulga rightly rejects her mother's shallow aphorisms and her disgustingly optimistic attitude. Hulga and her mother complement each other, each lacking what the other has in the extreme; thus, ironically, both of them are vulnerable to the truly evil opportunism of Manley Pointer, the Bible salesman. Readers might be sympathetic with either one of them, for there is some virtue in Mrs. Hopewell's generosity, just as there is in Hulga's unsentimental disdain.

The same antithesis is found between Mrs. Turpin in "Revelation" and the Wellesley girl Mary Grace, except that in this story the irony is more clearly resolved when Mrs. Turpin understands that her virtues (and her sincere, though misguided, consideration and generosity are in one sense very real virtues) are of no consequence in the context of eternity.

The problem of interpretation in Flannery O'Connor's fiction, then, is not a matter of choosing a good character over a bad one, or even of judging one bad character against a worse one. Her irony is referable to an extremely objective view of reality that discovers each man to be lacking in some fashion, grotesque in some way, a misfit in one sense or another; and yet it also finds that all of these inadequacies are insufficient grounds for excluding the character from compassion, especially in the derivative sense of this word, *suffering with*. Her irony is such that the reader has responded poorly if he does not feel revulsion as well as compassion for each of the principal figures and some of the minor ones. This is not a contention that there are no characters who function as clearly good or bad in the rhetorical sense, for it has been shown previously that certain figures are used to draw the issues decisively: the priests, Mr. Guizac, and the mental deficients on the one hand, and the Bible salesman, the homosexual, and Hoover Shoats on the other. There is no question as to their significance and no irony in their functions; but most of the major figures, even those as apparently lost as the Misfit and Enoch Emory, are ameliorated when considered in the context of Miss O'Connor's Christian irony.

In the novels, *Wise Blood* and *The Violent Bear It Away*, the irony is like that found in the short stories already discussed. It is not unusual, of course, for novels and short stories to lead an ignorant character to knowledge, a naive character to maturity, or a cowardly character to heroism. Nor is the picaro an unusual central figure. But in both of Flannery O'Connor's novels, the negative aspects of the main characters are especially pronounced. In *Wise Blood*, Hazel Motes's perverse pagan exuberance in the early portions of the novel leads the reader to classify him wrongly in one of two fashions: either Haze is heroic in publicly renouncing an empty religion which fosters superstition and hypocrisy; or Haze is a villainous antichrist, representing in a somewhat exaggerated backwoods fashion the general impiety and godlessness of the twentieth century. At the conclusion of the book, however, one realizes that Haze, even in the early chapters, is the moral norm against which other characters are measured; it is only through the positiveness of his presence that the satirical portraits have meaning. Asa Hawks, Enoch Emory, Sabbath Lily Hawks, and Hoover Shoats are characters fit to populate the Inferno; if Hazel Motes were not ultimately different from them, the novel would remain at the dead center of negativism. The ironic device leads the reader to conclude that the world the novel depicts is totally corrupt, showing him finally that his judgment failed to take into account the omnipresent possibility of melioration—theologically, the opportunity to accept grace. When Haze accepts this opportunity, the reader must then reconsider his character from the first and realize that the strength of character which enabled him to blaspheme at the top of his voice is the quality which led to his ultimate conversion. Early in the novel he serves a positive function in that the reader prefers his directness and honesty to the devious, cynical, and hypocritical behavior of the world at large; the reader's choice at this point, however, is a secular one. At the conclusion of the novel, the blasphemous positive figure from the early parts of the novel transcends his secular role and necessitates a choice between this world and the next. The irony has brought the reader, and the main character, from a sense of nothingness and despair to a Christian affirmation and acceptance of life. Yet the reader who is insensitive to the meaning of Mrs. Flood's conversion by the example of her tenant Hazel may continue to feel that the novel's main point is to present the ravaging effects of Haze's severely religious background and his resulting sense of outrage and guilt.

There is no resolution to this problem, for it is inherent in Flannery O'Connor's choice of reaching a small audience forcefully rather than a larger audience equivocally. Lewis A. Lawson suggests the liabilities of methods other than severe Christian irony:

[Flannery O'Connor] could have, then, chosen to narrate the story of a modern saint. But such a story would have had the quality of sentimental and intrusive moralism, of preaching, about it which would have alienated the very audience which she wanted to reach. She could have, then, chosen to analyze the rather normal man's attempt to establish a meaningful spiritual relationship in a world where disbelief, especially in the guise of belief, is rampant. But the trouble with this approach would be that the character might be so like his audience that it would not have perceived his problem. That leaves, then, the opposite of the saint: the active disbeliever. Here a demonic figure could have been constructed, but a demonic figure would be without the desire to believe in the first place, and so there would have been no conflict. The ideal figure, it seems, would be a saint who disbelieved, that is, one who was actively searching for religious meaning (as opposed to the majority who passively accept the traditional view, although they secretly regard it as nonsense) but who did not find it in the established beliefs.[11]

11. "Flannery O'Connor and the Grotesque: *Wise Blood,*" *Renascence,* XVII (Spring 1965), 145.

Tarwater, in *The Violent Bear It Away,* resembles
Hazel Motes in this regard, for in the bulk of the novel
he is a rebellious, disrespectful, willfully perverse character who actively attempts to deny everything that his
grandfather has taught him. Part of the irony is that he
tries just as hard to reject what Rayber wants him to
believe. As in *Wise Blood,* the reader is drawn between
two courses of action, either of which could be "right"
to an audience without clear understanding of its religious belief. Many readers (in fact the typical reader, if
there is any correspondence between the population at
large and the reading population) feels about this problem in much the same way that Mrs. McIntyre believes
in religion: Jesus is fine in church on Sunday but a
nuisance any other time. Flannery O'Connor's method
betrays those who would feel that Tarwater would
really be "better off" with Rayber because he would
become a reliable member of society by giving up the
"fanatical" religious notions of his grandfather. These
same readers would have some reluctance to give up
God altogether; Flannery O'Connor in this novel,
through her irony, forces her lukewarm readers to make
such a choice; if they choose what is "best for the boy,"
they are shockingly disappointed by the denouement in
which Tarwater baptizes Bishop, Rayber sinks into
empty despair, and Tarwater turns decisively toward
the mission which his grandfather had assigned him.
Such a "hero" is different from the picaresque hero in
that the reader is not amused or sympathetic with his
roguery—he is revolted by it or sympathizes with it for
the wrong reasons. And Tarwater is not an anti-hero,
either, for his negative qualities are implicitly reproved,

his protest fails, and he assumes a singularly positive Christian role at the end of the novel.

To speak of a concluding positive Christian theme is to suggest that Flannery O'Connor's stories and novels end with some sense of elevation, something akin to the conclusion of the *Divine Comedy* in contrast to the nature of the preceding grim subject matter. Such a feeling is indeed evoked in the novels and even in some of the stories which end in death, such as "A Good Man Is Hard to Find," "The River," "Greenleaf," and "Judgement Day." In certain other stories, the irony arises from a structure inverse to this comic pattern, beginning with an essentially comic or satiric focus and ending in tragedy. Although a Christian theme is nevertheless apparent, the final effect of such stories is decidedly tragic; "Everything That Rises Must Converge," "A View of the Woods," and "The Comforts of Home," are typical. The quality of irony which dominates the conclusion of these stories is that described by Northrop Frye in *Anatomy of Criticism:*

Such tragic irony differs from satire in that there is no attempt to make fun of the character, but only to bring out clearly the "all too human," as distinct from the heroic, aspects of the tragedy. King Lear attempts to achieve heroic dignity through his position as a king and father, and finds it instead in his suffering humanity: hence it is in *King Lear* that we find what has been called the "comedy of the grotesque," the ironic parody of the tragic situation, most elaborately developed.

As a phase of irony in its own right, the fourth phase looks at tragedy from below, from the moral and realistic perspective of the state of experience. It stresses the humanity of its heroes, minimizes the sense of ritual inevitability in tragedy, supplies social and psychological explanations for catastrophe, and makes as much as possible of human misery seem, in Thoreau's phrase, "superfluous and evitable." This is the phase of most sincere, explicit realism.[12]

In the opening portions of "Everything That Rises Must Converge" there is ironic tension between what each character would like to be and what he is. Julian's mother is poor but proud, overweight, and somewhat vain; like many other struggling widows in Miss O'Connor's fiction, she relies heavily upon aphorisms—in her instance, for the purpose of shoring up her dignity: rationalizing her son's indolence, she says, "You've only been out of school a year. Rome wasn't built in a day"; and later, "With the world in the mess it's in . . . , it's a wonder we can enjoy anything. I tell you, the bottom rail is on the top" (*Everything*, p. 6). She insists that Julian must recognize who he is and live up to his aristocratic background. Julian, on the other hand, maintains a superior attitude towards his mother and her opinions, telling her that "True culture is in the mind, the *mind*" (p. 9). Ironically, the arguments of each of these characters contain considerable truth, but neither argument is sufficient to achieve the intended heroic dignity. The curious combination of these two mutually inadequate dialectics brings about the tragic conclusion which renders the entire story an "ironic parody of the tragic situation." Although the characters are by no means heroic and there is a strong sense that the human misery is "superfluous and evitable," the tragic feeling is quite strong. The theme of the conclusion is Christian, but the epiphany comes not to

12. P. 237.

the mother in the agony of her death, but to Julian, who is left not only with broader knowledge of sympathy, charity, and true dignity, but also with the heavy burden of guilt for his own mother's death.

"A View of the Woods" is quite similar in its ironic catastrophe. In his own perverse manner, Mark Fortune seeks to preserve his dignity and identity as a Fortune by dominating the Pittses, and what he finds commendable in Mary Fortune, his granddaughter, is her resemblance to him. Secretly, her own sense of dignity is achieved by her faith to being a Pitts, in the name of which she accepts her role as scapegoat for her grandfather's spiteful behavior toward her family. The irony lies in the fact that her tantrum, which precipitates the tragic ending in which she and old Fortune kill each other, is evidence of the fierce pride of her Fortune blood rather than the adamant stoicism of her father; the very quality which her grandfather had nourished in her is the one which destroys both of them. Thus, in defending her identity as a Pitts she has become irrevocably a Fortune. The oppressive conclusion leaves the reader contemplating the terrible consequences of the culpability of both victims, not the grandness of passions heroically defended.

At the conclusion of "The Comforts of Home," Thomas stands above his mother's corpse. With him is Sarah Ham, the nymphomaniac who was brought into the home by Thomas's mother; the result of her misplaced charity is the rift in the family which ultimately brings about the disaster. When Sheriff Farebrother appears just moments after the mother has been shot, his analysis of the event points out part of the irony:

The sheriff's brain worked instantly like a calculating machine. He saw the facts as if they were already in print: the fellow had intended all along to kill his mother and pin it on the girl. But Farebrother had been too quick for him. They were not yet aware of his head in the door. As he scrutinized the scene, further insights were flashed to him. Over her body, the killer and the slut were about to collapse into each other's arms. The sheriff knew a nasty bit when he saw it. He was accustomed to enter upon scenes that were not as bad as he had hoped to find them, but this one met his expectations (*Everything*, pp. 141–142).

Neither analysis is correct, and both of them attribute to Thomas motives which, though criminal and abhorrent, would at least qualify him as a villain. As a matter of fact, Thomas fires as a consequence of the imagined advice of his father, a man of unscrupulous expediency whom Thomas despised during his lifetime:

Thomas had inherited his father's reason without his ruthlessness and his mother's love of good without her tendency to pursue it. His plan for all practical action was to wait and see what developed (p. 121).

His one practical action of firing the pistol goes awry, for he intended to shoot Sarah Ham, not his mother. Ironically, Thomas's isolated and single yielding to the principles of his father brings catastrophe; although he has overcome his habitual weakness in the matter of self-assertion, his victory is a defeat and a gratuitous tragedy.

This tragic irony is a means of illustrating the Christian theme once again in a somewhat different manner, for it provides a contrast between the pettiness and destructiveness of private, personal, limited concerns and the vast, overpowering, universal charity above them. The loss has been in the name of something transitory and inconsequential, and it is from the ironic sense of this disparity that the tragic effect is made.

Irony, though presenting a formidable barrier to interpretation, is essential to Flannery O'Connor's theme; for only through it is she able to present the staggering complexity of reality from a Christian point of view. In using such irony, she is not so indirect as to be obscure or ambiguous. Her approach to the subject matter is not predictable, is not the result of an ironic formula, for it has been shown that even though irony is an almost constant feature of her fiction, its results in terms of plot and structure vary according to the demands of the material. Both the content and the technique of her fiction attest to a belief that God writes straight with crooked lines; the crooked lines are the paradoxes, the grotesqueries, the experiential oxymorons, and the deceiving, complex ironies which she uses to express her persistent and inflexible Christian theme.

The difficulties that the typical Flannery O'Connor story presents are like those encountered in much modern poetry; both contain techniques that are oblique rather than direct; both seek to convey the total complexity of the subject without sacrificing the author's moral intent; and both employ a principle of economy which generates such density that only the serious reader can respond adequately to the work of art before him. To the literary dilettante, to the morally neutral reader, and to those who are squeamish or sentimental, Flannery O'Connor's fiction will generate a startling range of misconceptions and preposterous analytical abuses. But to the reader with a sound background in modern literature and an orthodox understanding of Christocentric religion, Miss O'Connor's work will be understood for what it is—a unique and forceful body of fiction based upon the profound and yet simple verities that have been the focal point of Western thought for almost two thousand years.

Bibliography

Attwater, Donald (editor). *A Catholic Dictionary*. 3rd ed. New York: The Macmillan Co., 1958.

Ballif, Algene. "A Southern Allegory," *Commentary*, XXX (October 1960), 358–362.

Baumbach, Jonathan. *The Landscape of Nightmare*. New York: New York University Press, 1965.

Cheney, Brainard. "Flannery O'Connor's Campaign for Her Country," *Sewanee Review*, LXXII (Autumn 1964), 555–558.

———. "Miss O'Connor Creates Unusual Humor Out of Ordinary Sin," *Sewanee Review*, LXXI (Autumn 1963), 644–652.

Coleman, Richard. "Flannery O'Connor: A Scrutiny of Two Forms of Her Many-Leveled Art," *The Phoenix* (College of Charleston), Fall-Winter, 1965–66, pp. 30–69.

De Vitis, A. A. *Graham Greene*. New York: Twayne Publishers Inc., 1964.

Dobrée, Bonamy. *English Literature in the Early Eighteenth Century, 1700–1740*. New York: Oxford University Press, 1959.

Drake, Robert. *Flannery O'Connor: A Critical Essay*. Grand Rapids: William B. Eerdmans, 1966.

Esty, William. "In America, Intellectual Bomb Shelters," *Commonweal*, March 7, 1958, pp. 586–588.

Evans, Oliver. "Spiritual Isolation in Carson McCullers," *South: Modern Southern Literature in Its Cultural Setting*, edited by Louis D. Rubin, Jr., and Robert D. Jacobs. Garden City: Dolphin Books, Doubleday & Co., Inc., 1961.

Farnham, James F. "The Grotesque in Flannery O'Connor," *America*, CV (May 13, 1961), 277, 280–281.

Ferris, Sumner J. "The Outside and the Inside: Flannery O'Connor's *The Violent Bear It Away*," *Critique*, III (Winter-Spring 1960), 11–19.

Fitzgerald, Robert. "The Countryside and the True Country," *Sewanee Review*, LXX (Summer 1962), 380–394.

Ford, Jesse Hill. "Vanderbilt's Literary Symposium: Program for Spectators," Nashville *Tennessean*. September 4, 1966, p. B-1.

Friedman, Melvin J. and Lewis A. Lawson, editors. *The Added Dimension: The Art and Mind of Flannery O'Connor*. New York: Fordham University Press, 1966.

Friedman, Melvin J. "Flannery O'Connor: Another Legend in Southern Fiction," *English Journal*, LI (April 1962), 233–243.

Frye, Northrop. *Anatomy of Criticism: Four Essays*. Princeton: Princeton University Press, 1957.

Gable, Sister Mariella, O.S.B. "The Ecumenic Core in Flannery O'Connor's Fiction," *American Benedictine Review*, XV (June 1964), 127–143.

———. Untitled contribution to "Flannery O'Connor—A Tribute," *Esprit* [University of Scranton], VIII (Winter 1964), 25–27.

Gordon, Caroline. "Flannery O'Connor's *Wise Blood*," *Critique*, II (Fall 1958), 3–10.

Hassan, Ihab. *Radical Innocence: Studies in The Contemporary American Novel*. Princeton: Princeton University Press, 1961.

Hawkes, John. "Flannery O'Connor's Devil," *Sewanee Review*, LXX (Summer 1962), 395–407.

"An Interview with Flannery O'Connor and Robert Penn Warren," *Vagabond* [Vanderbilt University], IV, No. 2 (February 1960), 9–17.

Joselyn, Sister M., O.S.B. "Thematic Centers in 'The Displaced Person,' " *Studies in Short Fiction*, I (Winter 1964), 85–92.

Lawson, Lewis A. "Flannery O'Connor and the Grotesque: *Wise Blood*," *Renascence*, XVII (Spring 1965), 137–147, 156.

McCown, Robert. "Flannery O'Connor and the Reality of Sin," *Catholic World*, CLXXXVIII (January 1959), 285–291.

Malin, Irving. *New American Gothic*, preface by Harry T. Moore. Carbondale: Southern Illinois University Press, 1962.

Nolde, M. Simon. "*The Violent Bear It Away*: A Study in Imagery," *Xavier University Studies*, I (Spring 1962), 180–194.

O'Connor, Flannery. "The Church and the Fiction Writer," *America*, March 30, 1957, pp. 733–735.

———. *Everything That Rises Must Converge*, introduction by Robert Fitzgerald. New York: Farrar, Straus & Giroux, 1965.

———. "The Fiction Writer and His Country," *The Living Novel: A Symposium*, edited by Granville Hicks. New York: The Macmillan Co., 1957.

———. "The Geranium," *Accent*, VI (Summer 1946), 245–253.

———. *A Good Man Is Hard to Find*. New York: Harcourt, Brace & World, Inc., 1955.

———. Letter to Andrew Lytle, February 4, 1960. Tennessee State Library and Archives, Nashville, Tennessee.

———. "Living With a Peacock," *Holiday*, September 1961, pp. 52, 110 ff.

O'Connor, Flannery. "The Partridge Festival," reprinted from *The Critic*, in *The Sense of Fiction*, edited by Robert L. Welker and Herschel Gower. Englewood Cliffs, New Jersey: Prentice-Hall, Inc., 1966, pp. 372–390.

———. *The Violent Bear It Away*. New York: Farrar, Straus & Cudahy, 1960.

———. *Wise Blood*. 2nd ed. New York: Farrar, Straus & Cudahy, 1962.

Peden, William. *The American Short Story*. Boston: Houghton Mifflin Co., 1964.

Poirier, Richard. "If You Know Who You Are You Can Go Anywhere," *New York Times Book Review*, May 30, 1965, pp. 6, 22.

Quinn, Sister M. Bernetta. "View from a Rock: The Fiction of Flannery O'Connor and J. F. Powers," *Critique*, II (Fall 1958), 19–27.

Rosenfield, Claire. "The Shadow Within: The Conscious and Unconscious Use of the Double," *Stories of the Double*, edited by Albert J. Guerard. New York: J. B. Lippincott Company, 1967.

Sartre, Jean-Paul. *Existentialism*, translated by Bernard Frechtman. New York: Philosophical Library, 1947.

Sister Bertrande. "Four Stories of Flannery O'Connor," *Thought*, XXVII (Autumn 1962), 410–426.

Sister Mary Alice. "My Mentor, Flannery O'Connor," *Saturday Review*, May 29, 1965, pp. 24–25.

Stelzmann, Rainulf. "Shock and Orthodoxy: An Interpretation of Flannery O'Connor's Novels and Short Stories," *Xavier University Studies*, II (March 1963), 4–21.

Stern, Richard. "Flannery O'Connor: A Remembrance and Some Letters," *Shenandoah*, XVI (Winter 1965), 5–10.

Teilhard de Chardin, Pierre. *The Phenomenon of Man*, translated by Bernard Wall, introduction by Sir Julian Huxley. New York: Harper and Brothers, 1959.

Van Doornik, N. G. M., S. Jelsma, and A. Van De Lisdonk. *A Handbook of the Catholic Faith*, translated anonymously from the Dutch, edited by John Greenwood. Garden City, New York: Image Books, 1956.

Varma, Devendra. *The Gothic Flame*. London: Arthur Barker, Ltd., 1957.

Wagenknecht, Edward. *Cavalcade of the English Novel*. New York: Henry Holt and Co., 1943.

Walston, Rosa Lee. "Flannery O'Connor—A Good Writer Is Hard to Find," *Columns* (The Woman's College of Georgia), Fall 1965, pp. 8–13.

Index